THE
CHICK MAGNET
COOKBOOK

THE
CHICK MAGNET
COOKBOOK

More Than Seventy Seductive Recipes
to Get Your Sex Life Sizzling

Garth Fuller

CITADEL PRESS
Kensington Publishing Corp.
www.kensingtonbooks.com

CITADEL PRESS BOOKS are published by

Kensington Publishing Corp.
850 Third Avenue
New York, NY 10022

All Kensington titles, imprints, and distributed lines are available at special quantity discounts for bulk purchases for sales promotions, premiums, fund-raising, educational, or institutional use. Special book excerpts or customized printings can also be created to fit specific needs. For details, write or phone the office of the Kensington special sales manager: Kensington Publishing Corp., 850 Third Avenue, New York, NY 10022, attn: Special Sales Department; phone 1-800-221-2647.

First printing: February 2004

10   9   8   7   6   5   4   3   2   1

Printed in the United States of America

Library of Congress Control Number: 2003106189

ISBN 0-8065-2568-1

To the last girl I cooked for:
Thank you for everything you've done.
You're more important to me
than you'll ever know.

Contents

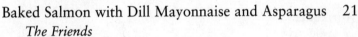

Cooking for All Occasions   93

Grilling   109

Salads   125

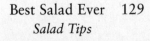

THE
CHICK MAGNET
COOKBOOK

Introduction

Why Should Men Cook?

We men do a lot in the name of pulling chicks. We buy them drinks in bars, sit through tear-jerking movies with them, and hold their purses while they try on pair after pair of jeans. Hell, we even pretend to listen to the endless stream of meaningless drivel that comes out of their mouths . . . all in the hopes that we might get some lovin'. And the lovin'; it seems, comes few and far between.

Wouldn't it be nice to find a foolproof way of getting some? A tried and tested method that makes chicks swoon? A veritable "finishing move"? A dating "crane kick" of sorts?

Enter the home-cooked meal.

Why Cooking for Chicks Works

Women are experts at sniffing out an ambush. They are quick to identify even the most cunning plan of conquest, and their purpose in life seems aimed at finding reasons why *you* should not be allowed to sleep with them. So why does cooking for chicks work? Why does it seem that women's defenses are rendered useless by food? Consider the following forces and factors at work.

Cooking As Romance

Chicks are starved for romance—starved for guys who show a little bit of creativity, effort, and style in their attempts to get laid. When you cook for a chick, these cravings are satisfied with fail-safe consistency. A candlelit table, a fantastic meal prepared by the man of her dreams, an after-dinner glass of wine by the fire; these are the

1

things women dream of. The classic go-to date of dinner at a restaurant followed by a chick flick is old, tired, and reeks of desperation. Cooking for a chick will show her you're an inventive, daring suitor, and that you're prepared to meet her romantic needs.

Cooking As Fantasy

Let us digress, for a moment, and talk about porn. Think back to the extensive research you've done on the subject and ask yourself, "Where do porn scenes traditionally take place?" The typical answer includes such standard settings for male sexual fantasy as locker rooms, nurses' offices, female penitentiaries, parking garages, etc.

Now consider your experience watching softcore porn; porn created with couples and female viewers in mind. In addition to the overwhelming frustration involved with the poor-camera-angle/head-in the-way/strategically-placed-shadow/no-money-shot cinematography, what do we notice about the setting? Gone are the restaurant bathrooms and shoe stores, absent are the parking structures and dungeons. In their place, the female forums for fantasy: log cabins, candlelit dinners, fireside cuddling, strawberry and champagne feedings, and the occasional breakfast nook thrown in for good measure.

When you cook for chicks, you're tapping into the same fantasy that softcore porn writers milk with so much ease—the domestication of men. Women dream about sitting next to the fire with men clad in flannel pajamas. They dream about men feeding them strawberries. They dream about quaintly decorated log cabins. They dream about, you guessed it, men preparing them a special, romantic meal. The lesson? Appear domesticated by cooking for a chick, and an all-access pass to female fantasy is yours.

Food As Status Symbol

Food is the ultimate background check, the premier credential evaluation. Indeed, the food we eat and enjoy can say a lot about who we are and, more important, what we know.

For instance, serving a dish that comes with crumbled potato chips baked on top sends a different message than does serving a dish that calls for a topping of garlic aioli. The former indicates that your culinary tastes were molded by all-you-can-eat buffets and disaster relief centers. The latter suggests that you have been outside your county line, that you know the difference between fine dining and volume shopping, and that you have an ounce of taste and class.

The beauty of cooking lies in that we can select foods that send her any number of favorable messages. We can prepare dishes for her that show we just might be the renaissance man of her dreams, even if we're really the furthest thing from it. Just because you're not a worldly, cultured gourmet ("complete barbarian" may be closer to the truth), doesn't mean you can't convey a sense of decorum with the food you serve. Taste and class tend to be high on a chick's "will I sleep with him?" checklist, and cooking a great meal will earn you a stellar review.

Food and Sex

We've all heard the old wives' tales concerning the sexual potency of certain foods. Tomatoes dull inhibition, chocolate arouses love, and pumpkin seeds bring a woman into heat. Oysters, perhaps the Holy Grail of aphrodisiacs, are said to promote legendary stamina in men.

Though the sexual effects of food may be overblown (no amount of shellfish will keep you from being a two-pump chump), the intimate link between food and sex cannot be ignored. For men, the link manifests itself in the post-coital beckoning of the refrigerator, when the caress of your mate pales in comparison to anything dipped in Ranch dressing. For women, the connection is reversed—food begets sex. Women love to eat first and have sex later. Cook her a great meal and she may see fit to include you in the second half of the equation.

Food Says, "I Care"

To prepare food for someone is to say, "I care about you." This understanding, food as affection, is a universal aspect of human nature. Yes, she'll be impressed that you know a little about food. Yes, she'll notice that you have taste and class. Yes, she will be seduced by the fantasy of male domestication. But most of all, she will be thrilled to death that you cared enough to cook for her.

"But Cooking Will Make Me Look Gay"

Yes it will . . . and chicks love gay dudes.

If you're like most guys, you regularly deplete your funds, exhaust your free time, and compromise your self-respect, all in an effort to get laid. Gay guys, on the other hand, turn down more ass than you'll see in two lifetimes. Taking a page out of their book might not be such a bad idea.

What You Should Cook for Chicks

The question of what to cook should not be taken lightly, and before we even look at recipes we have to lay down some ground rules concerning menu selection. The right dish will ensure that you fulfill her culinary and romantic desires, while the wrong dish can leave you embarrassed and doing the dishes alone. Whether cooking from one of the recipes in this book or experimenting with one of your own, the following rules and recommendations will minimize your chances of getting it wrong.

Never Cook Her Favorite Meal

So she says chicken fajitas are her favorite, she absolutely adores them. Sounds great, right? Wrong. Steer clear of anything even remotely resembling her favorite dish. Even though the majority of chicks in the world are not gourmet food critics, they can spot a poor excuse for their favorite foods. Stick to something she is less familiar with. That way, even if your dish doesn't come out perfectly, she won't know the difference.

Never Cook an Italian Girl Pasta

In fact, never cook a chick anything related to her cultural, ethnic, or geographic origin. Two reasons: First and foremost, you run the risk of being labeled an insensitive, stereotyping idiot (i.e., "Look Rosarita, I made you burritos, mixed you a margarita, and spread straw on the floor so that you would be more comfortable in my country!"). This approach will not get you laid.

Second, chances are a chick with a specific geographic or ethnic background can spot an amateur attempt at her national dish. Italian girls know pasta, Spanish girls know paella, and you don't know much about either. As mentioned earlier, leave yourself some room for error and go with what she doesn't know.

Leave the Meatloaf at Home

Same goes for lasagna, hamburgers, tuna casserole, etc. Every American family has their own tried and tested version of these dishes, and every American family is convinced that their version is the best. Any rendition of an ultra-traditional dish that you cook up will only fall short of Mom's recipe. Furthermore, nobody ever got laid by fixing a chick meatloaf.

Not All Chicks Like a Thick Piece of Meat on the First Date

Red meat and chicks often don't get along too well. For many girls, a big steak is simply too heavy and too dense. Not to say red meat should be avoided altogether, but the selection of cut, the manner of preparation, and the role beef plays in the dinner must be adjusted accordingly.

You should check with your date to make sure she's not a vegetarian. If she is, you need to ask yourself what the hell you're doing hanging out with a vegetarian. Sure, there's a small chance she's into new age massage, nudism, and tantric sex, but there's a 100 percent chance you'll first have to put up with dinner talk involving topics ranging from women's lib to Greenpeace.

When in Doubt, Ask

Getting initial clearance on your menu choice can save you from outright disaster. Don't give her the third degree, but feel free to bounce some ideas off her. "How does seafood sound?" "Mexican okay with you?" "Is chicken fair game?" "Care to dine in the nude?"

Drinks with Dinner?

Absolutely. Suddenly your jokes are a bit funnier, you become ever so slightly more attractive, and the food tastes like it was prepared by a seasoned gourmet. Behold the power of alcohol. In the right amount, drinks with dinner can truly complete the experience. Too much alcohol, however, and the evening can end up a complete disaster. Err on the side of moderation. This concept most certainly violates your usual mission statement regarding alcohol and chicks, but the evening will be better for it.

Drinks are only a small part of the equation. Smells, tastes, and conversation can weaken the knees more than even the strongest liquor, and taking care to present drinks as an accessory to your evening rather than the focus will work in your favor. That said, let's talk more about how beer, wine, and liquor can help make your meal a success.

"Let's See . . . I Have OE 800, Boone's Farm, and a Plastic Bottle of Vodka."

Malt liquor never hurt nobody. The problem is no chick on earth (or at least none that you want in your house) will be even remotely impressed by you serving drinks from a forty-ounce bottle. What we drink can say a great deal about who we are, or at least who we want chicks to think we are.

This is not to say you have to spend a fortune on alcohol, nor does it mean you have to become a sommelier overnight. A little forethought and a few tips can help cover all your bases in the drinks department.

The Beer Question

Many would argue beer simply doesn't cut it when it comes to fine food. That might have been true years ago, when mass-produced domestics were the final word. Today, the beer aisle is crowded with imports, microbrews, and specialty craft beers, all of which make cracking a brew at the dinner table a definite option.

Pairing beer and food is certainly no art form, and personal taste should have final say. Chicks, on the whole, tend to prefer lighter beers such as Hefeweizen, or even an occasional fruit-flavored beer (cherry lambics, raspberry ales, etc.). Make sure if you offer her a pear cider, that you have another type of beer on hand for yourself. However good you think it might taste, drinking a fruity beer will make you look like a complete candy-ass.

"A Perfect Nose, Kickin' Body, Delicious Fruit . . . and My Date Wasn't Half-Bad Either."

There is a truly staggering amount of information on wine. Advice concerning wine storage, wine tasting, wine and food pairing, and wine etiquette goes on and on. Wine lovers get so serious about all this crap, it makes you wonder if they've forgotten the original and most important function of wine: to make sure everyone gets laid.

There is really no need to fuss with all the intricacies of wine choice and etiquette, but familiarizing yourself with different types of wine and the proper methods of serving them can only make you look better in front of your date. You may even find that knowing a little bit about wine will help you enjoy it more. Keep in mind, however, that overdoing it with the wine lingo will make you look like a pompous loser with too much time on his hands.

For our purposes, we need only cover one rule in wine selection: Forget the rules. All the knowledge in the world is useless if you end up with a wine that neither you nor your date find very tasty. Though some recommendations are tossed around throughout this book, go with what you like and save the worrying for the food.

Before or After . . . Never During

Liquor simply doesn't go well with main courses. Too sweet, too bitter, too strong—it will always be something. Before and after, however, the gloves come off.

Unlike beer and wine, your taste buds should play absolutely no role in choosing which drinks to serve. Why? Because no matter how masculine you consider yourself to be, your tastes will certainly betray your better judgment. Before you know it you'll be mixing yourself a stiff Malibu and pineapple, and losing the respect of every female in sight.

If liquor is going to be an option at any point in the evening, you're probably going to have to provide two distinct choices, one male and one female. For yourself, stick to the big three of vodka, gin, or whiskey, and cut them 2 to 1 with a fruit-free mixer (lime wedges are acceptable). This leaves a wide array of drinks to work with, including scotch and soda, gin and tonic, and vodka collins, all of which maintain your manhood and taste pretty damn good too.

For her, break out the fruit. Vodka with cranberry and screw-drivers taste great and are easy to make. Fancier chick drinks such as amaretto sours and Long Island iced teas are usually a hit, but forget them. You'll have enough to worry about with dinner.

Some Cooking Basics

Like any artisans, chefs have a high regard for proper style and methodology in their work. For every slice of the knife, every turn of the spoon, there exists a time-honored technique to be learned and adhered to. For the amateur cook that cares more about landing chicks than proper whisking technique, much of this technical know-how can be regarded as industry and hobbyist nit-picking.

Without getting too serious, we can employ some professional skills and strategies that will certainly improve our ability to create great meals. The following are some general tips that will help you avoid some of the pitfalls confronting the novice chef.

Read the Damn Recipe

Perpetuated by sitcoms and commercials, the myth that guys don't read directions is difficult to shake. Whether or not it's true, when cooking for a chick you absolutely have to read the directions.

Cooking can be likened to alchemy, with ingredients interacting in mysterious ways to create completely unexpected flavors and tex-tures. Altering the timing, volume, or order of ingredient additions can drastically alter the end product. Therefore, reading the recipe with care before setting foot in the kitchen is a must. If you are read-ing a recipe for the first time while ingredients are already on the stove, your chances of getting laid will be burning up right along with your main course.

"Everything in Its Place"

The French write checks their ridiculous accents and silly moustaches just can't cash. They wouldn't have had a revolution without us, we saved their asses from the Germans—twice—and bailed them out of a nasty colonial uprising in Indochina. What have we gotten in return?

Well, the French may not know jack about sticking up for themselves, but they can teach us a thing or two about cooking. One French culinary tradition in particular, *mise en place* (pronounced *meez-on-ploss* and meaning "everything in its place"), will make a significant impact on your ability to pull off a great meal. To create a "meez," chop and/or measure all of your ingredients according to the recipe, and place them into small bowls. These bowls should then be arranged in the order in which they will be added to the dish.

The benefits of a good "meez" cannot be understated. The technique reduces the risk of being caught unprepared mid-recipe, and ensures that your ingredients will be added at the right time and in the right form. Essentially, you will reduce potential for error, and raise the odds your date will be served a perfect meal. Just think, every time you use *mise en place* to help you pull chicks, our forefathers' efforts in babysitting France seem a little more worthwhile.

Knife Work

As any professional chef will tell you, the knife is the most important piece of equipment in your kitchen. In the hands of the right person it can slice, mince, chop, crush, tenderize, and even create art. In the hands of the wrong person, the knife is a ticking time bomb, waiting to hurt and maim the operator, leaving a wake of unimpressed females in its path.

Scrapes that can be fixed by Band-Aids are cute and endearing. Knife cuts are rarely so. Proper knife technique is as much about safety as performance, so adhering to some basic principles just may save you from losing some flesh.

- *Go slowly.* You're not working in a 500-meal-per-night restaurant, nor are you competing in a timed cooking contest.
- *Use your knuckles to hold food and guide the knife,* keeping your fingertips out of harm's way.
- *If possible, give the food you are working with a flat edge.* This will keep the item from rolling or slipping while you cut it.
- *Practice.* Knife proficiency takes time, so don't be surprised if early efforts are awkward and time consuming.
- *Use a high-quality, very sharp knife.* Dull knives require more pressure and slip easily (a great combo for injury).

No Tank Tops

Fashion advice is beyond the scope of this text—what you wear to the dinner table is between you and whatever fashion gods you worship. In the kitchen, though, a few general maxims should be observed:

- *Do not wear loose fitting or bulky clothing.* Your dashiki will be dragging in the sauce and sweeping through the flame, so go with short or rolled-up sleeves.

- *Consider an apron.* But don't consider wearing it around your neck. Fold it at the waist like a waiter does.

- *No oven mitts.* I have yet to meet the girl that gets turned on by checker-print, terry-cloth lobster claws.

- *TV cool.* Watch most professional chefs on TV and you'll see that they have a clean dish towel draped over their shoulder. It's perfect for wiping hands, picking up hot cookware, or snapping your date's rear-end.

- *Wear shoes.* When that knife tumbles off the counter in slow-motion, headed straight for your metatarsals, you'll thank yourself for not going barefoot.

Use Fresh Ingredients

Using top-drawer ingredients can mitigate much of what you lack in cooking knowhow, and using the highest quality possible will have a noticeable effect on your finished product. Alternately, the use of poor ingredients can create taste and appearance disasters that are utterly impossible to recover from. Indeed, the greatest chefs on Earth, armed with the finest recipes the culinary world has to offer, can be rendered limp-dick by sub-par ingredients.

Though some specific ingredient choices are littered throughout the recipe section, the subject can be summed up by saying, "Buy everything fresh." Food that has been lying around too long, nursing off of preservatives, or living in a can simply won't taste as good as fresh, quality items. Second-rate ingredients are like dancers you meet at strip clubs and then take to your uncle's wedding—no matter how you cover them up, they're going to somehow make an ass of you and leave a terrible taste in your mouth.

Granted, the quest for fresh ingredients will force you to stray from that well-worn grocery store path between the hot deli and the beer aisle, but your dinner will be better for it. If in doubt, simply ask the produce guy or butcher to help you. Those guys are the nicest, most knowledgeable, arguably underpaid workers in the world, and they'll gladly help you find what you need.

And Without Further Ado . . . the Recipes

The concoctions in this book are not meant to be easy to make; real food takes real effort. None of them are beyond the reach of a novice, but all of them demand careful attention. Recipes for every imaginable girl, and every conceivable situation, lie ahead. Read closely, plan ahead, and success will be yours.

Dinner

Teriyaki Chicken Breasts with Yakisoba and Sunomono

Pat Morita notwithstanding, teriyaki has been Japan's most successful and widely acclaimed export, and with good reason. The version that follows is so good, you'll have to use Daniel San–esque moves just to keep her off you. Wax on, brother.

 DRINKS

Dishes with a high salt content (including most Japanese food) will tend to eclipse all but the most acidic wines. A German riesling, which is highly acidic, will be best suited to cut through the teriyaki.

A medium-strong lager such as Sapporo Dark will work equally well.

 INGREDIENTS

Most grocery stores carry fresh ginger (do not use powdered). Yakisoba (Japanese noodles) can be bought dry or fresh—either way, follow the directions on the package and you'll get good results. Fresh, shiny, and firm chicken breasts are a must.

FOR THE SUNOMONO
- 1 large cucumber, peeled and sliced into ⅛-inch-thick rounds
- 2 green onions, finely chopped
- ¼ cup rice vinegar
- 1 tablespoon sesame oil
- 1 tablespoon soy sauce

FOR THE YAKISOBA
Two packages yakisoba (four servings), dry or fresh

FOR THE CHICKEN BREASTS
- 3 boneless chicken breasts, skin on or skinless

 This icon indicates any cooking steps that can (or should) be done ahead of time.

FOR THE SAUCE

1 cup soy sauce

1 cup granulated sugar

1 4-inch piece fresh ginger, peeled and sliced thin

3 cloves garlic, crushed and peeled

2 tablespoons bourbon whiskey

 ## For the Sunomono

1. Combine all ingredients in a bowl. Taste and adjust accordingly.
2. Place in refrigerator until ready to serve.

 ## Making the Sauce

1. In a small saucepan over medium heat, stir soy sauce and sugar together until sugar is dissolved.
2. Add ginger, garlic, and bourbon and bring to a boil. Reduce heat and simmer (sauce should be barely bubbling) for about 30 minutes, stirring occasionally.
3. Remove large pieces of ginger or garlic from sauce.

Baking the Chicken

1. Preheat oven to 325 degrees F.
2. Place chicken in a baking dish and baste with teriyaki sauce.
3. Bake for 30 minutes or until no longer pink inside, basting every ten minutes. Do not overcook. A meat thermometer should read 160 degrees F when inserted into the center of the breast.
4. When chicken is nearing completion, begin cooking yakisoba. (Noodles should be just finishing when chicken is removed from oven.)

Making the Yakisoba

Follow directions on packaging (omit vegetables). Serve hot from skillet.

Serving

Drizzle remaining sauce over chicken and place next to equal portions of sunomono and yakisoba.

Perfect Breasts

Dry, tough, and flavorless, overcooked chicken breasts have become an all-too-common affliction of American-male cuisine. The blight is so widespread that few guys would recognize plump, juicy breasts that aren't attached to girls named Crystal, Cheyenne, or Cinnamon. Luckily, there are ways to bring well-prepared breasts to your table that don't involve a ten-dollar cover charge.

To start with, make sure you're using breasts of even thickness. With breasts of uneven thickness (abandon the boob metaphor here), the interiors of the cuts will never be done at the same time. When the thicker breast is just right, the thinner will be well on its way to overcooking. To remedy this, simply pound the thicker cuts with a roller, kitchen mallet, or wine bottle until they are all of uniform thickness.

Once on the stove or in the oven, you can use a meat thermometer to determine the precise moment when your chicken is ready to serve. Inserted into the exact center of the breast, a thermometer should read 160 degrees F at proper doneness. This temperature is hot enough to kill any nasty bacteria (applies only to poultry, not strippers), and low enough to leave you with perfectly done chicken. Used together, these two techniques will give you perfect breasts every time.

Pasta Carbonara

This is one dish you may not want to cook for a steady girlfriend or spouse. The high fat content will have you cringing every time she goes back for another helping . . . unless, of course, you plan on working off the calories together. Rich, decadent, and comically easy to prepare, this dish makes a great short-notice charmer.

 DRINKS

A soft, creamy chardonnay will mirror this dish perfectly. Steer clear of highly acidic wines such as most rieslings.

Moretti, an Italian lager-style beer, will make an equally nice accompaniment.

 INGREDIENTS

Any corner grocery should have all you need for good carbonara. Score the highest-quality parmigiano-reggiano you can find, and remember, excellent cheese rarely comes pre-grated, and never comes in a green canister.

FOR THE PASTA
½ pound fresh spaghetti or angel hair

FOR THE CARBONARA
2 large egg yolks, beaten
2 tablespoons heavy cream
½ teaspoon salt
¼ pound bacon

3 teaspoons finely chopped garlic
1 teaspoon freshly ground black pepper
½ cup freshly grated parmigiano-reggiano
1 tablespoon fresh parsley, finely chopped

Cooking the Pasta

1. Fill a large pot with water. Add pinch of salt if desired. Bring to boil over high heat.
2. Add pasta and follow cooking instructions on package for al dente pasta (just barely done, not overcooked).
3. Drain in a colander. Set aside.

Making the Carbonara

1. Whisk egg yolks, cream, and salt in a small bowl and set aside. Place a large sauté pan or stockpot over medium heat. Once hot, cook bacon until crisp.
2. Remove bacon and pat dry with paper towels. Chop into small bits and set aside.
3. Pour off all but approximately 3 tablespoons of bacon fat. Return pan to heat and add garlic along with black pepper. Sauté for 30 seconds.
4. Return bacon to pan and add pasta. Sauté for 1 minute, stirring frequently.
5. Remove from heat and immediately add egg mixture, stirring quickly until eggs begin to thicken.
6. Add cheese and stir.

Serving

Getting this dish served as soon as it's ready is key. Immediately after the cheese is blended, garnish carbonara with parsley and get it to the table. Find some great bread and serve it with two tablespoons of olive oil to one tablespoon of balsamic vinegar drizzled on a small plate.

Candlelight

To the female mind, anything and everything is made more romantic when done by candlelight. Even simple, everyday tasks like bathing and reading can take on an air of sexuality in the presence of a soft flame. Eating dinner is no different, and candles should not be left off the evening's to-do list. There's no single way to employ candle power, but the following recommendations should be considered:

- *Don't use scented candles.* The "vanilla-mint bliss" candle that hides the ball-sweat smell in your bedroom should stay right wear it is. Bringing sickeningly sweet scents and flavors to the table will only confuse her palate and make the food taste like a urinal puck.

- *Long for elegant, short for casual.* If you're presenting the evening as an elaborate, fancy affair, use long candles in candlesticks. If the evening is a casual dinner for two, use a shorter, thicker, freestanding candle.

- *Don't overdo it.* Placing twenty-five candles in the kitchen, on the table, and in the bathroom will make you look like you're trying too hard (or holding a séance to resurrect your dead sex life). One candle on the table is the perfect understatement.

- *Don't use a lighter.* Unless you're serving the deer she shot and cleaned today, use matches like a civilized human being.

Baked Salmon with Dill Mayonnaise and Asparagus

Salmon, asparagus, and mayonnaise form one of the great trios of western cuisine—a ménage à trois that you actually get to witness in person instead of hearing about from your luckier-than-hell buddy. But who knows? Serve to the right pair of guests, and the three-part harmony might not stop at the table.

 DRINKS

A chardonnay may be your best bet for this dish. The creamy flavor of the wine will balance the mayonnaise nicely.

Salmon is a fish made for beer. A hearty lager or ale with citrus tones will complement the fish well.

 **INGREDIENTS**

Finding fresh salmon is a must—avoid brown flesh and look for firm, bright orange fillets with shiny-scaled skin. Wild salmon will possess a deeper, more complex flavor, while farm-raised fish will be lighter. Best Foods mayonnaise will work as well as any other. (If you were thinking Miracle Whip, go to the far end of the double-wide and await your punishment.)

FOR THE SALMON

2 8-ounce salmon fillets, bones removed, skin on or off (have your fishmonger prepare the fillets for you)

Salt and pepper to taste

2 tablespoons mayonnaise

6 sprigs fresh dill

1 lemon cut in half crosswise

FOR THE DILL MAYONNAISE

½ cup mayonnaise

2 tablespoons fresh dill, finely chopped

juice from ½ lemon

FOR THE ASPARAGUS

1 bunch fresh asparagus, tough ends snapped off

7 ounces (½ can) chicken broth

Making the Dill Mayonnaise

1. Combine mayonnaise, chopped dill, and lemon juice in a small serving bowl. Mix together until a smooth consistency is reached.
2. Keep covered in the refrigerator until ready to serve.

Baking the Salmon

1. Preheat oven to 325 degrees F. Rinse fillets, pat dry with a paper towel, and season lightly with salt and pepper.
2. Lightly coat both sides of the fish with plain mayonnaise.
3. Lay sprigs of dill on top of fillets, and squeeze the juice of one lemon over both.
4. Wrap in tin foil and seal the ends.
5. Bake for 10–12 minutes, or until moist and flaky.

Braising the Asparagus

1. Place asparagus and chicken broth in a medium-sized sauté pan.
2. Bring broth to boil over high heat. Reduce heat and simmer for 3 minutes.

Serving

The dill mayonnaise can be served on the side or as a thin top coat for the salmon; regardless, bring the extra to the table. Fresh sourdough bread will round out the meal nicely.

The Friends

They don't think you're funny. They hate the way you dress. They criticize your every move. And right now they're trying to set her up with some guy they know from the gym. Clearly, her friends are not your friends.

But they *can* be put to good use. Invite your chick and a few of her friends over for dinner, and those would-be saboteurs can be converted to first-class disseminators of pro-you propaganda. Serve them some good eats, and she'll soon be hearing your praises sung by the people whose opinions matter more than her own.

Need another reason to cook for her friends? Simple: You'll be laying a stellar foundation for the post-breakup, "friends of the ex" dating spree. Now *that's* cooking with gas.

Chimichangas

Chimichangas are not traditional Mexican food, but rather a border adaptation using common Mexican ingredients. The crispness of the fried tortilla, the smoothness of the filling, and the freshness of the garnish make this dish great. An easy meal to prepare, chimichangas look great and are guaranteed to impress.

Much of the prep work can be completed before the cooking begins, leaving only the frying of the chimis to worry about. For this dish, proper frying is key, so make sure you're free of distractions and ready to go before you heat the oil.

 DRINKS

Many wines can't handle the alternately smooth, citrus, and spicy flavors of border food. A good zinfandel will have the best chance.

Mexican food and beer is a match made in heaven. Skip the Corona and go with a beer of substance such as Bohemia or Negra Modelo.

 INGREDIENTS

Because chimis are so simple and many of the components are served raw, make a special effort to find quality ingredients (lettuce, for instance, does not grow in a sealed bag). Pay special attention to finding great tomatoes for the salsa, and the freshest tortillas available. If at all possible, get your tortillas from a tortilleria or restaurant that makes them fresh daily.

FOR THE GARNISH
2 cups chopped lettuce

Fresh cilantro leaves, torn off stem

1 cup cheese, preferably crumbled Mexican Cotija, or shredded sharp cheddar

½ cup sour cream

FOR THE SALSA

1 can Rotel tomatoes and green chilies

2 roma tomatoes or one regular tomato, chopped

1 bunch green onions, sliced

juice from one lime

FOR THE CHIMIS

1 can refried beans

½ cup shredded sharp cheddar

4 flour tortillas

Creating the Garnish and Salsa

1. Chop lettuce, tear cilantro, grate cheese, and spoon out sour cream. Place all four on a serving plate, dividing the plate into quarters.
2. Mix salsa ingredients and place in a serving bowl.
3. Cover garnish and salsa and place both in refrigerator until ready to serve.

Making the Filling

1. Place refried beans in a small saucepan over low to medium heat. Stir in cheddar cheese until thoroughly melted. Reduce heat and keep warm until ready to use, taking care not to let beans stick or burn.

Frying the Chimis

1. Place frying pan over medium to high heat. Once pan is heated, fill with oil to a depth of around ⅛ of an inch. If oil begins to smoke at any time, it's too damn hot.
2. While oil is heating, heat tortillas in microwave between two plates for 15 seconds.
3. Remove one tortilla and place three tablespoons of filling on tortilla, slightly off center. Fold as you would a burrito with closed ends.
4. Place folded tortilla in the oil, seam side down. Turn when lightly browned (about 40 seconds). Continue to turn, browning all sides evenly.

5. When done, remove chimi from oil and place on paper towel. Pat dry with towel.
6. Repeat for remaining tortillas.

Serving

The best way to serve chimis is buffet style. Just place the garnish and salsa on the counter, present her with a plated chimi, and she can top it as she sees fit. If you want, serve Spanish rice on the side. (The Spanish rice you make from a box will turn out better than any recipe you attempt.)

Food Smells

Ideally, the cooking process should be well under way by the time your date arrives. That way the fantastic odors escaping from your masterpiece in progress will work her into a frenzy of appetite and anticipation—an olfactory foreplay, if you will. By the time she sits down to eat, her curiosity will have been piqued and her defenses will be weakened.

Food scents can be powerful aphrodisiacs and memory triggers, but only if you let them work uninterrupted. Therefore, while both cooking and eating, avoid introducing powerful extra-culinary scents into the equation. The subtle hint of cologne or the gut-wrenching reek of cigarette smoke can ruin a meal faster than anything, so guard against them with vigilance.

As for the post-meal festivities, be equally leery of introducing your own "blend of spices" to the atmosphere—a threat made even more serious when dishes like the one above are served. If you are notoriously ill equipped to digest foods such as refried beans, skip them altogether. Or, if you must, keep a bottle of Beano handy, *and* hidden—only discoveries of anti-fungal cream or German fetish videos will end a date faster.

Roast Chicken with Red Onions

Of roasting the perfect chicken, *The Joy of Cooking* says, "Consider the bird ready when the uppermost part of the thigh exudes clear juices." Damn straight!

Sexual metaphor notwithstanding, roasting a chicken is tougher than you think. The darker, richer thigh meat tends to cook slower than the lighter breast meat, and by the time the former is done, the latter is often dry and overcooked. But by eliminating the pesky breast and focusing on the more flavorful thighs and legs, this recipe puts great roast chicken within reach. Throw in some fresh herbs, add some onions along the way, and with relative ease you'll have the juices flowing in no time.

 DRINKS

The intense herb flavors of this dish will demand a fragrant, herby wine such as pinot gris. Some pairing guides suggest serving white zinfandel or rosé with chicken—please don't.

When serving beer with chicken, the more malt the better. Choose a rich golden lager with deep tones.

 INGREDIENTS

The supermarket will carry numerous grades of chicken in various states of disassembly. You'll need roaster or free-range thighs and legs, with the skin left on. Go to the produce aisle and pick out the freshest, most fragrant bundles of thyme and parsley. Dried herbs are not an option.

FOR THE CHICKEN

- 4 roaster or free-range chicken thighs with legs, attached or separated
- 2 tablespoons butter, divided into 8 knobs
- 1 cup chopped parsley leaves
- 1 cup thyme leaves (pulled off stem)
- Salt and freshly ground black pepper to taste

FOR THE RED ONIONS
  4 small to medium red onions
  2 tablespoons butter, divided
     into 4 pats
  4 sprigs of thyme

Preparing the Chicken for Roasting

1. Preheat the oven to 425 degrees F, and lightly coat your roasting pan by smearing a pat of butter with a paper towel along the bottom and sides of the pan.
2. Gently separate the skin from the meat of each piece of chicken, leaving the outer borders attached. This will create a pocket in which to stuff butter and herbs. Lightly salt the inside of the pocket.
3. Gently push one knob of butter and a pinch each of the parsley and thyme into each one of the pockets.
4. Arrange the chicken in the roasting pan, skin side up.

Preparing the Onions for Roasting

1. Peel onions. Slice off bottom ⅛ of each onion, creating a flat surface on which each can rest.
2. Use a small knife to carve out a rounded depression (½-inch deep) on the top of each onion, providing a "dish" for the butter and herbs. Then use a knife to slice the onion nearly into quarters. Do not slice through completely. Onion should remain intact, with slices allowing for melted butter to seep through.
3. Into each rounded depression, press one ½ tablespoon pat of butter, along with one stem of thyme.
4. Set onions aside. You will add them to the roasting pan shortly.

Roasting

1. Place chicken in oven. Cook for 10 minutes, then add onions. Distribute the onions evenly among the chicken pieces. Return the pan to the oven.
2. Chicken is done when the poke of a sharp knife yields clear running juices, around 40 minutes. Alternatively, a meat thermometer should read 170 degrees F when inserted deep in the thigh.

Serving

Serve chicken and red onions alongside one another, with warm bread as an accompaniment.

Pink Wine

A plague has taken hold of the American male. It is a terrible affliction that causes otherwise virile men to behave like complete pansies. More widespread than the onyx-stone tuxedo tie, more noticeable than Sun-In, more devastating to testosterone levels than the Mazda Miata, behold . . . the awful specter of pink wine.

When you reach for a glass of shimmering pink vino, you effectively fire off a giant, pink flare for all vessels to see. The message, loud and clear, is one of poor taste and wavering sexual identity. Chicks will run, as well they should.

Enthusiasts and aficionados alike declare afternoon summer picnics to be the appropriate forum for wines such as rosé and white zinfandel (so feel free to bring them to your next football tailgater). Otherwise, leave the undermining of your masculinity to your poor performance in bed.

Pan-Fried Halibut over Wasabi
Mashed Potatoes with
Baby Bok Choy

Asian flavors, bistro-like preparation, and unique colors make this dish a definite lady killer. The name alone is sexier than you'll ever be. Not all chicks will take a liking to wasabi, so check to see if she's into the hot, green stuff.

 DRINKS

Wasabi, like its American cousin, horseradish, will wreak havoc on most wines. An assertive sauvignon will have the best chance of standing up to the strong flavor.

Beer may be a better option. The fresh, flowery taste of a pilsner will complement the rawness of the wasabi without overpowering the halibut. The Czech beer Pilsner Urquell makes a great choice.

 INGREDIENTS

Dashi, or bonito soup-stock, comes in powder form and can be found at any Asian market. Grab some wasabi at your local supermarket sushi bar.

FOR THE POTATOES

- 4 Russet potatoes
- ⅛ cup whole milk
- 2 tablespoons butter
- 1 tablespoon wasabi paste
  Salt to taste

FOR THE SAUCE

- 2 cloves garlic, chopped
- 2 teaspoons chopped ginger
- ½ cup dashi
- ¼ cup soy sauce
- ¼ cup sake
- ¼ cup mirin (Chinese rice wine)
- ½ teaspoon cornstarch dissolved in 1 tablespoon cold water

FOR THE FISH

  2 6-ounce halibut steaks

  1 tablespoon sesame oil

FOR THE BOK CHOY

  4 to 6 baby bok choy

  1 can chicken broth

 ## Making the Mashed Potatoes

1. Peel and cut potatoes in half. Place them in a large pot with water to cover, and bring to a boil over high heat.

2. Potatoes are done when they slide off an inserted fork, about 15 to 20 minutes. Err on the side of overcooking them; you don't want raw potato chunks in your mash.

3. Drain the potatoes and add the remaining ingredients right to the pot. Blend all ingredients evenly. *Important*: Don't over-beat the potatoes. Overbeating releases starches that create a glue-like consistency.

4. To keep warm until serving, place potatoes in the oven at about 150 degrees F. Stir occasionally to avoid burning.

Making the Sauce

1. Combine all ingredients in a small saucepan over medium heat. Bring to a boil, then reduce heat and simmer for ten minutes.

2. Add cornstarch solution and stir until sauce comes to a slow boil. Thicken only slightly, just until the sauce coats the back of a clean spoon. Keep the sauce warm until serving.

Frying the Fish

1. Place frying pan over medium-high heat. When pan is heated, coat with 1 tablespoon of sesame oil.

2. Rinse halibut, then pat dry with paper towel and season lightly with a pinch or two of salt.

3. Fry halibut until golden on each side and moist and flaky, about 5 to 7 minutes.

Cooking the Bok Choy

1. Wash bok choy and place in a pan. Fill pan with chicken broth to a depth of about ⅓ inch.
2. Bring chicken broth to a boil. Reduce heat and cover, simmering for around two minutes. Drain and serve.

Serving

Start with a bed of mashed potatoes only slightly larger than the halibut steaks. Place a steak in the middle of the bed, and two or three bok choy on the side. Drizzle the sauce over the entire plate. Watch as your chicky drizzles affection over you.

Music

Music creates mood. It can send a distinct message, establish ambiance, and provide a soundtrack for your perfect evening. It can also fill those painfully long gaps in conversation.

But don't just press the "random play" button. Put some thought into choosing the score. The following tips should help steer you in the right direction:

- *No Barbra Streisand, Cher, or showtunes.* Cooking will not make you look gay. Cooking while humming along to *Funny Girl* will.

- *Don't pair ethnic dishes with like-ethnic music.* You're cooking her a romantic meal, not opening a theme restaurant.

- *No classical.* Unless it's part of your known repertoire, classical music will make you look like you're trying too hard.

- *Hold off on the Marvin Gaye.* The "Let's Get It On" bomb should not be dropped until you're within point-blank range of the target, if at all.

Pot Roast

If women share one fantasy in common, it's the "after-dinner glass of wine in front of a fireplace on a cold winter's night." But the dinner comes first, and no meal is better suited to a snowy evening than pot roast.

The one-pot nature of this meal makes it a no-brainer, and this recipe will yield much more than you need (tomorrow's pot roast sandwiches during the game). But remember, pot roast takes hours to cook, so get an early start.

 DRINKS

The deep, stocky flavor of pot roast begs for a sturdy red wine. Go with a cabernet sauvignon or merlot.

Likewise, an ale with more pronounced flavors will work well. Try the hoppy, complex Sierra Nevada Pale Ale.

 INGREDIENTS

Ask the butcher for a boneless rump roast. (Don't wink at him while asking.) Once you've got one, take the time to find fresh herbs.

FOR THE POT ROAST

- 2 tablespoons olive oil
- 3-to-4-pound boneless rump roast patted dry
- 2 celery stalks, chopped
- 1 yellow onion, chopped
- 1 tablespoon minced garlic
- 2½ cups canned beef stock
- ½ cup red wine
- 2 bay leaves
- 3 carrots, peeled and sliced into half-inch rounds
- 2 Russet potatoes, peeled and sliced into half-inch slices
- 1 tablespoon parsley, minced
- 1 tablespoon rosemary, minced
- 2 tablespoons green onions, chopped
- 1 teaspoon cornstarch dissolved in 1 tablespoon cold water

Browning Roast and Sautéing Vegetables

1. Heat a large pot over high heat. Add olive oil, swirling to coat the bottom.
2. When oil is hot, place roast in pot. Cook until golden on all sides.
3. Remove roast and set aside. Add celery, onion, and garlic to pan. Sauté until tender, around 2 to 3 minutes.
4. When vegetables are tender return beef to pan and remove from heat. Add beef stock, red wine, and bay leaves.

Cooking the Roast

1. Preheat oven to 300 degrees.
2. Place lid on pot and put in the oven. Roast for 2½ hours, basting meat every ½ hour. At this point, meat should be tender enough to pull apart and shred with a fork.
3. Remove pot from oven, but leave oven on. Remove roast from pot and set on a plate.
4. Remove and dispose of any large pieces of celery, garlic, and onion with a slotted spoon. There should be about 3 cups of liquid remaining; if less, add more stock and wine.
5. Return roast to pot, along with carrots and potatoes. Return to oven and cook for 45 minutes more.
6. When done, remove meat, carrots, and potatoes from pot.

Making the Sauce

1. Stir fresh herbs and green onions into pot and place on the stove over medium high heat. Bring to a slow simmer.
2. Stir in cornstarch and continue simmering, stirring occasionally, for 5 minutes.

Serving

Slice meat as thin or thick as she likes. Arrange on plate with vegetables, and pour sauce over all. Serve with plenty of warm sourdough bread.

Small Bites

Hors d'oeuvres, or "starters" as they are increasingly known, play a unique role in the world of the dinner date. Women have long used them as a crude, gold-digging litmus test; "If he orders them in a restaurant, then he knows how to treat me right." Thus, somehow, a giant onion dipped in batter and exploded in hot oil came to actually improve your chances of getting laid.

When cooking at home, hors d'oeuvres shoulder less dramatic impact. Instead, they can be used as they were intended— to whet the appetite and encourage her to bring an early glass of wine to her lips. Both effects will set the stage for your main course.

You'll easily have enough to worry about with dinner, so lean toward the simple. Top fresh mozzarella with tomato and basil, and drizzle with good olive oil. Dip hot bread in balsamic vinegar and olive oil. And when serving Asian food, stop by your favorite sushi joint and pick up a roll to go.

Pork Tenderloin with Balsamic Vinegar and Fennel

Rich and full of deep flavors, this one-pan dish is perfect for cool, autumn evenings. Though the preparation involves a good number of steps, none of them are difficult to execute. The only trick? Making sure you avoid all potentially inappropriate food puns. ("Speaking of pork tenderloin . . .")

 DRINKS

Vinegar has a high acidity that can leave many wines tasting flat. Serve an equally acidic wine such as a riesling for best results.

Red ales fit perfectly with pork. Killian's Irish Red will suffice, but try finding a craft-brewed red for best results.

 INGREDIENTS

Using a good bottle of balsamic vinegar will dramatically improve your end result. Look for one in the ten-to-fifteen-dollar range.

Shallots are small members of the onion family, and fennel (sometimes called anise) is a vegetable with a delicate licorice-like flavor. Both are available in most supermarkets.

1 pork tenderloin, 10 ounces or more	2 shallots, sliced into thin rounds
Salt and pepper to taste	4 tablespoons balsamic vinegar
1 tablespoon olive oil	3 teaspoons fresh sage, finely chopped
1 tablespoon unsalted butter	
2 fennel bulbs, sliced into ¼-inch strips	⅓ cup unsalted or low-sodium chicken broth

Browning the Pork

1. Preheat oven to 425 degrees F. Lightly season all sides of pork with salt and pepper.

2. Place an oven-proof pan on the stove over medium heat. When warm, add oil and butter.

3. When butter is melted and pan is hot, place pork in pan. Heat for 3 to 4 minutes on each side until evenly browned. Remove pork from pan and set aside.

Adding the Fennel

1. In the same pan, add the fennel and shallots. Continually stir until fennel is tender and golden brown, around 6 minutes.

2. Add 1 tablespoon of the balsamic vinegar and cook for 2 minutes, stirring constantly.

3. Turn off heat and stir in 1 teaspoon of fresh sage.

Reintroducing the Pork

1. Place the pork back into the pan, directly on top of the fennel. Sprinkle remaining sage over all.

2. Place in the oven and roast for 17 to 19 minutes.

3. Remove from oven and set pork aside, under foil, on a cutting board.

4. Remove fennel and shallot from pan and place on a plate. (You will return the mixture to the pan shortly.)

Adding the Broth

1. Place same pan over medium heat once again.

2. Add broth and remaining balsamic vinegar to pan.

3. Bring mixture to a boil over high heat, and cook until the liquid is reduced in half. Remove from heat.

4. Return fennel and shallot to pan and toss with liquid.

Serving

On the cutting board, slice pork into ½-inch-thick medallions. On each plate, arrange three or four medallions over a large spoonful of fennel. Garnish with sage if desired, and serve warm bread at the table.

The Invite

If your prospective dinner guest is someone you're dating regularly, then an invite to dinner will be seen for what it is—a charming, romantic liaison. If your prospective dinner date is a first-time player in your game, that same invite will be seen for what *it* is—a charming, romantic pre-game to sexual conquest on your home court.

Like William Wallace in a vengeful rage, chicks can smell an ambush a mile off. Therefore when inviting a chick to a home-cooked meal for two, how you ask becomes extremely important. While no fail-safe formula for the invite exists, the phrase "bring your toothbrush" should certainly be left out.

Remember to keep all invitations to dinner casual and fun— the less formality, the more relaxed she'll be, and the less pressure on you. How? Simply mention that you'd "like" to cook in her presence, and she'll be setting the date herself.

Coconut Shrimp with White Rice

A tip you won't find in Martha Stewart's *Living*—when handling jalapeño peppers, be sure to wash your hands before moving on to delicate male and female body parts. You think it hurts when you rub your eyes?

Potential for excruciating pain aside, this Thai dish has something for everyone. The aroma of coconut, the spiciness of fresh peppers, and the warmth of sherry make this dish a true pleaser.

 DRINKS

A smooth wine will best complement the sweetness created by the coconut. Try a creamy chardonnay for best results.

Earlier, we discussed the heinous nature of malt liquor. The Thai beer Singha is a notable exception, and it can be found in Asian markets and specialty beer stores.

 INGREDIENTS

Fresh shrimp will be shiny, firm, and without spots. They should also smell like deep, clean ocean water.

FOR THE SHRIMP

½ pound medium to large raw shrimp

3 teaspoons cornstarch

½ teaspoon salt

2 tablespoons dried coconut, unsweetened

2 tablespoons cooking oil

1 tablespoon butter

1 tablespoon minced garlic

2 small jalapeños, one red and one green

2 green onions, minced

1 tablespoon sherry, dry or cream

1 tablespoon soy sauce

½ teaspoon sugar

FOR THE WHITE RICE

1 cup white rice

Water to cover

Prepping the Shrimp

1. Tear off shell and legs, leaving tail intact. Use a sharp knife to slice the back of the shrimp open from head to tail. Using the tip of the knife, remove the black vein that has been exposed. Rinse shrimp under cold water.
2. Place shrimp in bowl. Add cornstarch and salt. Stir to coat shrimp. Let stand for 8 to 10 minutes. While shrimp is standing in cornstarch, begin steaming the rice.

Steaming the Rice

If you're going to eat rice more than once per year, invest in a rice cooker. They're inexpensive, easy to use, and extremely handy. Otherwise, follow the directions below.

1. Place washed rice in a small saucepan. Fill pan with water until rice is barely covered.
2. Set on high heat and bring to boil. Reduce heat to low, cover with lid, and simmer about 20 minutes or until all water has been absorbed by rice (while rice is cooking, continue with the shrimp).
3. Fluff rice with a fork and let stand 1 minute before serving.

Toasting the Coconut

1. Place coconut in wok (or sauté pan) over low heat. Cook and stir occasionally until golden brown.
2. Remove from wok and set aside.

Stir Frying Part I

1. Place wok over high heat until hot. Add oil and coat sides.
2. Add shrimp and cook for 2½ minutes, or just until shrimp is pink.
3. Remove the shrimp and set aside.

Stir Frying Part II

1. Reduce heat to medium. Add butter and coat sides of the wok.
2. Add garlic and cook for 1 minute.
3. Add jalapeños and onions. Cook for about 2 minutes.
4. Add sherry, soy, sugar, and coconut. Return shrimp to wok as well.
5. Dish is ready when final ingredients and shrimp are heated through.

Serving

Couldn't be easier. Put it on a plate, and serve the rice with Thai sweet chili sauce (available at many grocery stores).

Catholic Girls

Shrimp are the hot little Catholic girls of the sea—they can go very bad, very easily. But instead of raised hemlines and heavy petting behind the auditorium, bad shrimp bring poor taste, unpleasant texture, and guaranteed nausea.

When looking for fresh shrimp, your eyes and nose are the only guides you need. Fresh shrimp, like fresh fish, should look clean and smell like deep, cool ocean water. Shrimp on their way to reformatory school have a distinct ammonia-like odor, and may have black spots on their surface. When in doubt ask the fishmonger, and don't serve them if they seem iffy.

Browned Butter Chicken Cutlets
with Shallot and Mustard
Mashed Potatoes

Can you remember the last time you only had to put in twenty minutes of work to score with a chick? We thought not.

The simple richness of this dish doesn't suffer for the short preparation time, and what she doesn't know won't hurt her. Tell her it took you an hour . . . hell, two hours. In the end, she'll be glad that *some* of the work you did this evening lasted more than five minutes.

 DRINKS

Almost any of your favorite white wines will pair nicely with this dish. For something a little bit different and unexpected, try a very young pinot noir.

Brown, malty beer will go well with the chicken and browned butter. Newcastle Brown Ale and Samuel Smith Brown Ale top the list for taste and availability.

 INGREDIENTS

A chicken cutlet is simply a chicken breast sliced into two. Use Yukon Gold potatoes for the mash, and take care to find a high-quality Dijon mustard.

FOR THE POTATOES
- 8 Yukon Gold potatoes
- ½ cup vegetable oil
- 3 shallots, sliced as thinly as possible
- ⅛ cup whole milk
- 2 tablespoons butter
- 1 tablespoon mustard
- Salt to taste

FOR THE CUTLETS
- 3 boneless, skinless chicken cutlets
- Salt and freshly ground black pepper to taste
- ¾ cup flour for dredging
- 3 tablespoons vegetable oil

FOR THE TOPPING

1 to 2 tablespoons butter

2 tablespoons minced parsley
leaves

1 fresh lemon, quartered

 ## Making the Mashed Potatoes

1. Peel and cut potatoes in half. Place them in a large pot with
   water to cover, and bring to a boil over high heat.
2. Potatoes are done when they slide off an inserted fork, about
   15 to 20 minutes. Err on the side of overcooking them—you
   don't want raw potato chunks in your puree.
3. While the potatoes are boiling, heat the ½ cup of vegetable oil
   in a small frying pan over medium-high heat. When oil is hot,
   add shallots and fry until golden brown, about 2 to 3 minutes. Remove with a slotted spoon and pat dry with paper
   towels. Set aside.
4. Drain the potatoes, making sure *all* traces of water are
   removed. Add milk, butter, mustard, and salt right to the pot.
   Using hand mixer, ricer, or masher, blend all ingredients
   evenly. *Important*: Don't overbeat the potatoes—you'll end
   up with glue.
5. Potatoes can be made ahead of time and then reheated in the
   oven or on the stovetop over low heat. To avoid burning
   them, warm slowly on low heat and stir occasionally.
6. Mix in fried shallots just before serving.

Cooking the Chicken

1. Sprinkle both sides of chicken with salt and pepper. Place
   flour on a plate.
2. Heat a frying pan over medium-high heat until hot.
3. Add vegetable oil to cover bottom of pan in a thin layer. Let
   oil heat.
4. Dredge each chicken breast in flour, pressing the flour into the
   chicken to ensure contact.

5. Shake off excess flour and gently place breasts into oil. Cook on first side 3 to 5 minutes or until golden brown. Turn and cook on second side 2 to 3 minutes or until golden brown. When done, a meat thermometer should read 160 degrees when inserted into the center.

6. Remove cutlets from oil and drain briefly on a paper towel.

Browning the Butter

1. Melt the butter in a small saucepan over medium heat.

2. When butter begins to turn nut-brown (2 to 3 minutes), remove from heat.

Serving

Sprinkle parsley over cutlets and squeeze the juice from each lemon quarter over each. Just before bringing to the table, drizzle the browned butter over the top. Serve potatoes on the side.

Dishes

If your date's a keeper, she'll probably offer to do them. Politely decline and say, "I'll do them later." If she insists, suggest that the two of you do the dishes together. Be a gentleman and take control of the washing duties—leave the drying to her.

Teaming up on the dishes will give you a great opportunity to enjoy another glass of wine over a fun, laid-back activity. And with all that hot, foamy water flying around, who knows, someone might "accidentally" get splashed (your money move in high school). If nothing else, you'll be showing her that you're willing and able to take on the miserable task of dishes . . . which may dull her rage when, months later, you yell from the living room, "Stop clanging the dishes, I can't hear the TV!"

Seared Tuna Steaks with Roasted Garlic and Corn Mashed Potatoes

A properly seared tuna steak is a thing of beauty—a true standard bearer in the world of classy cuisine. When done right, the colors and textures alone will have her swooning. Overcook it, though, and you might as well have picked out two cans of tuna in spring water.

When searing, make sure you have the rest of the meal ready to go and are completely undistracted. Searing tuna is a delicate business and, unlike the nodding and smiling and "uh-huh"s that placate your date, the tuna will need your complete, undivided attention.

 DRINKS

Most red wines bring out an oily, metallic taste in tuna and should be avoided. Your favorite white wine should work here, but an Alsace riesling would be particularly nice.

With its flowery hop flavor, an India Pale Ale would complement this dish well. Look for a locally micro-brewed IPA.

 INGREDIENTS

Don't even attempt this dish if you can't find great tuna (i.e., the best you can afford). Asking the fishmonger for sushi-grade tuna is a good start.

Look for high-starch potatoes such as Yukon Gold for mashing.

FOR THE ROASTED GARLIC
  8 cloves unpeeled garlic
  1 tablespoon olive oil
     Freshly ground black pepper
     Aluminum foil

FOR THE POTATOES

- 6 Yukon Gold potatoes
- ¼ cup whole milk
- 2 tablespoons butter
- Salt to taste
- 1 small yellow onion, chopped
- ¾ cup corn kernels
- 1 tablespoon vegetable oil

FOR THE TUNA

- 2 tuna steaks, 6 to 8 ounces each
- 2 tablespoons freshly ground black pepper
- 2 tablespoons olive oil
- salt to taste

 ### Roasting the Garlic

1. Preheat the oven to 425 degrees F. Lay garlic in the middle of an 8-inch square piece of tin foil. Drizzle olive oil on top and add fresh ground pepper to taste.
2. Close foil around garlic and roast in the oven for 40 minutes. Remove garlic and allow to cool.
3. Squeeze each clove to extract the softened garlic. Set aside for later addition to the mashed potatoes.

 ### Making the Mashed Potatoes

1. Peel and cut potatoes in half. Place them in a large pot with water to cover and bring to a boil over high heat.
2. Potatoes are done when they slide off an inserted fork, about 15 to 20 minutes. Don't undercook, but don't let them get mushy, either.
3. Drain the potatoes and add the roasted garlic, milk, butter, and salt directly to the pot. Mash evenly until smooth. Remember: Don't overbeat. Keep warm in an oven set to 150 degrees.
4. Place frying pan over high heat. When hot, add oil and swirl to coat bottom and sides.
5. Add onions and cook, stirring occasionally, until onions are translucent.

6. Add corn and brown only slightly, about 2 to 3 minutes.

7. Add corn and onions to potatoes, taking care not to crush kernels.

8. Keep warm until ready to serve by placing in an oven warmed to 150 degrees.

Searing the Tuna

1. Rinse and pat steaks dry and coat with black pepper. Season with salt to taste.

2. Heat a sauté or frying pan over high heat. When pan is hot, add olive oil and swirl to coat the surface.

3. Sear tuna on one side for 2 minutes, or until golden. Turn and sear opposite side for 1 to 2 minutes. Remove from heat and serve. *Don't* overcook. Tuna should be bright red in the center (medium rare).

Serving

Form a bed of mashed potatoes in the middle of each plate. Place tuna steak directly on middle of bed.

Botch-Job

The asparagus lies limp on the plate, smelling like a urine-soaked dorm mattress. The oil fire in the kitchen has filled your apartment with black smoke. And the wine tastes like grape Kool-Aid mixed with vodka. You screwed the pooch . . . but you're still very much in the game.

When cooking for a chick, make sure you have a backup plan to cover any culinary disasters. The plan should be simple, laid-back, and fun, rescuing your chick from both the ruined meal and the potential awkwardness that comes with it. Pour another glass of wine, order Chinese and, most important, have a good laugh at yourself. Remember, handling a setback with style and good humor will impress a chick every bit as much as the perfect meal.

Filet Mignon with Red Wine Sauce and Baked Potato

There's a lot in a name. Simone is the sexy foreign exchange student. Abby is the tomboy cutie. Sarah is quiet and elegant. Alex, while downright hot, can be a real bitch. And filet mignon is the Cadillac of steaks, accessible only to professionals.

Not so . . . it's just meat (the filet, that is), and you can cook it without a culinary degree. Follow this recipe, taking care not to overcook the steaks, and all the luxury associated with "the cut" can be, in a word, *de rigueur*.

 DRINKS

Break out the good stuff. Cabernet and merlot are the natural choices.

Some people would argue that beer isn't "fancy" enough for filet. Wash down a bite with good golden ale to see why they're wrong.

 INGREDIENTS

Filet is expensive wherever you go—just make sure you're paying for fresh, bright meat. Finding a tawny port (a color distinction) will be best, but any dark port will do.

FOR THE BAKED POTATO
- 2 large Russet potatoes
- Tin foil for wrapping
- Butter
- Sour cream

FOR THE STEAKS
- 1 tablespoon olive oil
- 2 5-ounce filets
- Salt and pepper to taste

FOR THE SAUCE
- 3 tablespoons minced shallots
- ⅓ cup tawny port
- ⅔ cup red wine
- 1 cup canned beef broth
- 1½ teaspoons Dijon mustard
- 1 teaspoon cornstarch dissolved in 1 tablespoon water

Baking the Potatoes

1. Preheat oven to 425 degrees F.
2. Poke holes in potatoes with a fork. Wrap both potatoes separately in tin foil.
3. Bake for 50 to 55 minutes.

Cooking the Meat

1. Pat steaks dry with a paper towel. Season with salt and pepper. Heat a large, heavy skillet over high heat. Add oil.
2. Place filets in pan and brown for about 3 minutes on each side, just until medium rare.
3. Remove from pan and place on a plate. Cover with aluminum foil.

Making the Sauce

1. Add shallots to the skillet (leave drippings in). Sauté until soft.
2. Add port and red wine. Boil the mixture until it is reduced by two-thirds.
3. Add beef broth. Boil again until mixture is reduced by half.
4. Add mustard, whisking in with a fork. Bring to a boil, then add cornstarch mixture.
5. Reduce heat and maintain a low simmer. Stir until sauce thickens, around two minutes.
6. Add any juices that have accumulated under the steaks to the sauce and stir.

Serving

Slice filets into ¼-inch-thick medallions. Fan them on the plate, and drizzle sauce over the top. Make a slit in the top of the potatoes; serve accompanied by butter and sour cream at the table. A small dinner salad on the side would do nicely.

A Word for the Evening

de rigueur (**duh-rĭ-GRR**) *adj.* The norm, commonplace, the status quo.

When you're cooking great food for a chick, everything should be *de rigueur*. At your place, steaks are seared medium rare. Wine is sipped from stemware. Bread is buttered in small pieces, rather than all at once. Knives are on the right. And decent meals are cooked for attractive, appreciative females. No big deal. No fuss. Nothing special.

Keeping this air of *de rigueur* will win you points in a couple of ways. Having been shown that a nice, home-cooked meal is par for the course, your chick will be chomping at the bit to see your definition of special treatment. She'll also assume behaving in a civilized manner is the norm for you. Sure, the fact that you would just as soon pair Old Milwaukee with Hot Pockets as cabernet with lamb chops will eventually be exposed, but by then she'll find it charming rather than barbaric.

Chicken Adobo

Spain, the Philippines, Hawaii . . . each place consistently yields smoking hot chicks. In addition, each place features some form of Adobo in the local cuisine. In theory, if it's good enough for the beautiful women of these locales, it's good enough for the chicks in your hamlet. Indeed, you'll be hard pressed to find a girl that doesn't take to the sweet yet tart flavors of this tender chicken.

 DRINKS

The high acidity of this dish means that you'll have to match it with an equally acidic wine, say a dry, tart sauvignon blanc.

For beer, the sweetness of a nut brown ale is preferred to the bitterness of hop-laden beers. Try Newcastle Brown Ale or Samuel Smith's Nut Brown Ale.

 INGREDIENTS

You must use either rice vinegar or palm vinegar for this dish. *Do not* substitute any other type of vinegar. (See the text following this recipe for a warning about ingredient substitutions.)

FOR THE MARINADE
- 1 cup rice or palm vinegar
- ¼ cup plus 1 tablespoon soy sauce
- 1½ bay leaves
- 1 tablespoon minced garlic
- 1½ teaspoons sugar

FOR THE CHICKEN
- ¾ cup water
- 4 chicken legs and thighs (separate or joined)

FOR THE SAUCE
- 2 teaspoons cornstarch
- 1 tablespoon cold water

Marinating the Chicken

1. Combine ingredients of marinade in a large, heavy-bottomed pan. Add chicken and stir to coat.

2. Let sit for 40 minutes at room temperature, stirring occasionally.

Cooking the Chicken

1. Add ¾ cup water to the chicken and the marinade. Bring to a boil over high heat. Once boiling, reduce heat, cover, and simmer for 45 minutes.
2. When done, remove chicken from pot and set aside.

Making the Sauce

1. Return marinade to a boil.
2. Dissolve cornstarch in tablespoon of water. Add to marinade, stir, and reduce heat to a simmer.
3. Cook until sauce thickens. (When thickened, sauce should coat the back of a spoon.)

Serving

1. Return chicken to sauce. Stir to coat.
2. Serve with heaps of steamed rice. Lightly drizzle sauce over chicken and rice.

No Substitutions

Take James Bond. Replace his shaken (not stirred) martini with a Red Bull and vodka. Swap his perfectly tailored tux for a Men's Warehouse three-piece. Trade his Aston Martin in for a Mazda Miata. What do we have? Just another cheese-dick Englishman trying to peddle his accent for sex.

Clearly, messing with the parts can disrupt the effectiveness of the whole, and never is this more true than when cooking. The physical changes and chemical reactions that take place between ingredients are vital to your finished product, and messing with the reactants can be a disaster. "Corn meal, corn starch, who gives a . . ." until, that is, you actually taste your Frankensteinian concoction.

The business of ingredient substitution is a delicate one. If you find yourself short of a particular ingredient, check the internet for some tried and tested ingredient substitutions. Better yet, ask the good-looking girl that just moved next door if she can spare some.

Risotto with Pancetta and Peas

Extremely flexible, risotto can perform the culinary equivalent of pinning its ankles behind its ears. Seafood, beef, vegetables, innards, whatever—all can be tossed into a risotto. Or you can leave it plain and serve it as a side dish. Either way, make sure you treat risotto like you would a high-maintenance woman—don't take your eyes off it and keep it moist at all times.

 DRINKS

Because you can put anything in a risotto, the wine you choose might be dictated by the main ingredient. For a starting point, Pinot Grigio will do nicely.

Moretti, an Italian lager, will wash down risotto with the best of 'em.

 INGREDIENTS

Arborio rice, with its shorter grains and high starch content, is an absolute must. Without it, you won't have risotto. Pancetta is a spiced, cured ham that closely resembles bacon. Don't you dare use Parmesan from a green canister; use fresh grated only. The vermouth should be dry . . . and while you're at it, mix yourself a nice martini.

4 cups canned low-sodium chicken stock	14 ounces arborio rice
1 tablespoon olive oil	Salt and freshly ground black pepper
5 shallots, finely chopped	2 cups dry vermouth
2 cloves garlic, finely chopped	5 tablespoons butter
4 tablespoons diced pancetta	¾ cup freshly grated Parmesan
½ celery stalk, finely chopped	

1. Heat stock in a saucepan over medium heat and keep hot until ready to use.

2. Place a sauté pan over medium-high heat. When hot, add olive oil, swirling to coat sides. When oil is hot, add shallots, garlic, pancetta, and celery. Cook and stir for 3 minutes.

3. Add rice to sauté pan and season quickly with salt and pepper. Turn up heat to high. Rice will begin to fry, so make sure you are stirring it constantly. Cook rice in this manner for 1 minute.

4. Add vermouth and keep stirring. The rice will eventually absorb the liquid. When it does, continue to next step.

5. Turn down heat to medium. Add a dash of salt and one soup ladle full of hot stock to the rice while stirring constantly. Adjust heat so that stock is at a high simmer. When first ladle is absorbed, add a second, stirring constantly. Repeat process until all of stock is absorbed.

6. Remove from heat and check rice for doneness. It should be soft but slightly al dente. If it is undercooked, heat more stock and continue the process to completion. If done, continue to next step.

7. Add butter and Parmesan. Stir gently to avoid crushing rice. Place lid on pan and let rest for 3 minutes. *Do not remove lid for 3 minutes.* This is the time when the risotto is absorbing the butter and cheese. Eat immediately after lid is removed.

Specialty

A scenario: You choose a dish, and cook it for a certain chick. The meal is a success, and you reap the benefits. A short time later you make the dish again, for a different bird but with similar results. By now you're on a roll, and the third victim slayed by your ever-strengthening recipe doesn't even stand a chance. You've found a specialty—the dish that makes the hoop ten feet wide, the left-field fence close enough to spit at, and the opposing defense move in slo-mo.

The temptation would be to mine the mother-lode for all it's worth, to keep on with your newfound specialty until either the world supply of halibut or the world supply of chicks is exhausted. This, however, would be a mistake—all it takes is one exchange between your new chick and an ex (i.e., "He cooked his special halibut for you, didn't he?") and the game's up.

Girls are funny. They'll accept and even appreciate the fact that you have a past that involves sleeping with other girls. But they'll be genuinely upset to learn that you've cooked your special meal for other chicks ("I thought that was *our halibut!*"). The same can be said for songs, romantic restaurants, etc. Therefore, save your specialty for truly special moments, and keep the menu varied to avoid any backlash.

Sweet and Sour Chicken Soup

Takeout restaurants have substantially perverted the institution of "sweet and sour." The accepted version, according to purveyors of fried rice and tardy delivery, involves fluorescent pink sauce heaped onto pieces of dubious meat fried in batter. Here, at least, the "sweet and sour" refers simply to the unique balance of simple flavors achieved by this soup.

 DRINKS

Asian flavors can be tough to handle for most wines, so be sure to choose a powerful vino. For this dish, meet the strong flavors with a sauvignon blanc.

A light lager such as Kirin or Tsing Tao will prove wonderfully refreshing with this dish.

 INGREDIENTS

The recipe calls for rice vinegar, but palm vinegar will work, too. If you can't find somen (Japanese wheat noodle), use angel hair pasta. Finally, shiitakes are large mushrooms with a unique texture and flavor. Make an effort to find some, as they will really complete the dish.

6 cups canned low-sodium chicken stock

2 tablespoons rice vinegar

2 tablespoons soy sauce

1½ teaspoons minced garlic

1 teaspoon minced ginger

½ teaspoon salt

⅛ teaspoon freshly ground black pepper

1¾ cups thinly sliced shiitake mushrooms, stems removed

2 chicken breasts, cooked and shredded (you can do this in a skillet)

2 cups thinly sliced spinach leaves

1½ ounces uncooked somen noodles

1. In a large stockpot, combine chicken stock, vinegar, soy sauce, garlic, ginger, salt, pepper, and mushrooms. Bring to a boil over high heat.

2. Once boiling, reduce heat and bring mixture to a simmer. Cover and cook for 30 minutes to allow the flavors to combine. Stir occasionally.

3. Stir in chicken, spinach, and noodles. Simmer for 5 more minutes.

4. Serve with steamed rice on the side.

Prepping Home Court

Rest assured, she'll be going over your humble abode with a fine-tooth comb. Accordingly, condom stashes, skid-marked underwear, and pictures of ex-girlfriends during their overweight phase should be removed from view. A light dusting and a vacuuming wouldn't hurt, either.

But the only thing worse than leaving your bachelor pad a mess is trying too hard to make it look like Don Juan's love lair. If she spots rose petals on the bed, a bathtub filled with candles, and a care package of sex toys on her side of the bed, she may rightly regard the evening as a setup. Clean up, but let the food set the atmosphere and your charm convey the romance . . . okay, one out of two ain't bad.

Tarragon and Vinegar Chicken

How does a population of mustachioed, beret-wearing, deodorant-phobic men amass a reputation as great lovers? Could it be the food? One whiff of the odors escaping from this single-pot French dish and you'll start to think it might be. Serve it with warm French bread and the Gallic love equation will be complete (minus, we hope, the unshaven female participant).

 DRINKS

Choosing wine that will match the acidity of the vinegar will be a good place to start. Try a red sancerre (from the French region of the same name, made from the Pinot Noir grape).

Chicken and golden malt beers form a great pair.

 INGREDIENTS

Go to your butcher and ask for bone-in chicken breasts. Leaving the bone in will help maintain some of the flavor and moisture that chicken breasts so often lose. Sherry is a fortified wine ("Hey! Just like Maddog 20/20!") that can be found in any cooking store. For better quality try a wine shop. Use fresh tarragon, not dried. Finally, crème fraîche is a thickened cream that can be found in most gourmet grocery stores.

4 bone-in chicken breasts
  Salt and freshly ground black pepper
2 tablespoons olive oil
10 shallots, peeled and halved
10 pearl onions (blanched in boiling water, then peeled)
4 cloves garlic, peeled and halved

2 tablespoons fresh tarragon leaves
½ cup plus 2 tablespoons sherry vinegar
1³⁴ cups medium-dry sherry
1 tablespoon plus 2 teaspoons crème fraîche

Browning

1. Season chicken with salt and pepper. Place a large skillet over medium-high heat. When hot, add oil and swirl to coat sides.
2. When oil is hot, add 2 chicken breasts and fry quickly until surface is golden brown. Remove to a plate, then repeat procedure with remaining breasts.
3. When second batch of chicken is removed from pan, add shallots. Fry and stir until slightly browned. When shallots are just beginning to brown add pearl onions and garlic. Stir until garlic is only slightly browned (about 1 minute). Lower heat and move on to the next stage.

Simmering

1. Return chicken breasts to pan. Distribute tarragon leaves evenly over the chicken. Pour in vinegar and sherry.
2. Raise heat to bring mixture to a simmer, then reduce heat so that it is barely bubbling.
3. Let mixture cook in this manner for 25 minutes. At that time, turn chicken pieces over. Cook for another 20 minutes.
4. When done, remove chicken, garlic, shallots, and onions to a plate using a slotted spoon.

Finishing and Serving

1. Using a whisk, mix crème fraîche into sauce. Add salt and pepper if necessary. When desired flavor is reached, pour sauce over chicken.
2. Serve with plenty of warm, country-style bread for sopping.

Dinner and a Movie

If she doesn't attack you immediately following the meal, throw on a movie to keep her in the game. The late-evening video, after all, is really just a stalling tactic. You haven't yet made your move, but want to ensure she stays in your lair for at least another 103 minutes. That's all fine and good, but make sure you consider the following pieces of advice concerning post-dinner movie viewing.

- *The countdown.* As the minutes tick by on the VCR counter, your chances of scoring are slipping. She's got a full stomach, she's on a comfy couch, and thoughts of deep sleep are slowly replacing thoughts of you. Act now, my son.

- *No chick flicks.* You just cooked her dinner. She already thinks you're a caring, sensitive guy. Pouring on the *Sleepless in Seattle* will make you look a little too soft.

- *Don't press play.* Never use the play button to check what's already in the VCR. A full-screen shot of Jenna Jameson's funbags will probably end the evening.

- *Check the competition.* Two hours of Matt Damon and Ben Affleck on the screen will *not* have her realizing how lucky she is to end up with you. Choose a movie with a less desirable leading man, like Richard Dreyfuss.

- *Movie taste says a lot.* If your favorite movie is *Labyrinth, Navy Seals,* or anything involving a trilogy, you may never get laid. Grow up and move out of your parents' basement.

Morizqueta

Generally, low-fat means low taste, and low taste means low chick-pulling potential. Morizqueta, a traditional dish of mainland Mexico, represents a rare and welcomed exception. It's a healthy, low-fat meal that will impress with its simple preparation and great flavors. Cook it for the diet-obsessed girl who can't have fun if she thinks she's gaining weight. Or if your significant other has been gaining weight recently, get her hooked on Morizqueta. Everybody wins.

 DRINKS

If calories are really a concern, don't skip the drinks—eat less so you can drink more. Morizqueta is Mexican comfort food, perfect for a beer. A lager-style brew is your best bet, but almost any beer will do. Dos Equis is fine, but Bohemia will be even better.

Because the flavors in this dish are rather subtle, your wine options are fairly open, though a young zinfandel seems an obvious choice.

 INGREDIENTS

Quality tortillas, fresh tomatoes for the salsa, and fresh cilantro are key. Queso anejado (cotija) is a crumbly Mexican cheese that can be found in most large grocery or ethnic food stores.

FOR THE SALSA
- 1 can Rotel tomatoes and chilies
- Juice of 1 lime
- 2 green onions, chopped
- 2 roma tomatoes, chopped

FOR THE MORIZQUETA
- 2 cups steamed white rice (no "minute rice," slacker)
- 1 can black beans

FOR THE GARNISH
- 1 cup fresh cilantro leaves
- ¼ cup queso seco
- Flour or corn tortillas

Making the Salsa

Combine all ingredients in a bowl and mix. Refrigerate until serving.

Making the Morizqueta

1. Steam rice according to directions on package.
2. When rice is ready, heat black beans over medium-low heat until warm.

Serving

1. Spoon equal parts rice and beans onto two plates (rice first so as to create a base, then the beans on top of the rice).
2. Top with a layer of salsa and garnish with fresh cilantro. Crumble a tablespoon or two of queso seco over the top. Serve with heated tortillas on the side.

Appetite

No matter who the chick is, one of two things must be true—she either thinks she's fat, or she *is* fat. Because the evening's plans revolve around food, she may at some point go fishing for a reason to get upset, and she's sure to use you as the barometer.

The bait could be as simple as a post-meal, "Oh, I should not have eaten that much," or "Did I eat more than you?" Essentially, she's probing for your assessment of her ass size, and how you respond to these verbal snares can determine whether the evening ends in you crying out for joy or her crying on the floor.

The goal is to avoid any and all discussions regarding her weight, appetite, or eating performance. This can be accomplished by simply redirecting her comment toward yourself and repeating it with greater enthusiasm (i.e. "No way! *I'm the one who shouldn't have eaten that much!*"). Hopefully your empathy will be enough for her to drop the subject. If not, and she pursues the issue further, you're screwed. The best you'll manage is reserved heavy petting with the lights off.

Steak au Poivre and Homemade Oven Fries

Usually, fire in the kitchen is a bad thing. In this dish, however, the blue flames created by the addition of brandy to a hot pan are sure to wow even the coldest of fish. Approach the big moment casually and without fanfare. Just make sure she's watching. If your hair catches fire, you'll need her to lay a little stop, drop, and roll on your stupid ass.

 DRINKS

Red, red, and more red. A cabernet sauvignon will match the spiciness of the pepper and handle the richness of the meat.

A great beer dinner, steak and fries can be enjoyed with almost any brew. The smoothness of a light lager will be great for quenching the thirst brought on by the pepper and fries.

 INGREDIENTS

Tonight might be the night to hunt down some dry-aged, premium steaks. The aging process breaks down proteins in the meat, making it more tender. For the brandy, use a better than average bottle (let price be your guide).

FOR THE FRIES

- 3 tablespoons vegetable oil
- 2 tablespoons butter
- 4 Idaho potatoes, sliced into ⅛-inch wedges
- Salt and pepper
- ½ teaspoon garlic powder

FOR THE STEAK

- 2 6-ounce rib eye steaks
- Salt
- ½ cup Dijon mustard (reserve extra for sauce)
- 1 cup cracked black peppercorns
- 1 tablespoon oil

FOR THE SAUCE

¼ cup plus 1 teaspoon minced shallots

2 tablespoons brandy

1 tablespoon chopped garlic

2 cups canned low-sodium beef stock

¼ cup heavy cream

3 tablespoons salted butter

1 tablespoon vegetable oil

Making the Fries

1. Preheat oven to 400 degrees. Place a large skillet over high heat. When hot, add oil and swirl to coat sides.
2. Add butter and stir until melted. Add potatoes and stir to coat.
3. Cook for 10 minutes, stirring and tossing occasionally.
4. Transfer potatoes to a baking sheet, season with garlic powder, salt and pepper, and place in oven at 400 degrees for 20 minutes, or until golden brown.

Making The Steak

1. Preheat oven to 350 degrees. Season both sides of steak with salt. Brush steak with mustard, setting aside extra for later addition to sauce. Press peppercorns onto steak.
2. Heat a sauté pan over high heat. Add oil, and when oil is just starting to smoke, add steaks to pan. Cook for 3 minutes on each side.
3. Remove steaks from pan and place in a small baking pan or pie tin. Roast in oven for 8 minutes, or until medium-rare.

Making the Sauce

1. Place a sauté pan over medium-high heat. Add oil. When hot, add shallots, stirring and cooking for one minute.
2. USE CAUTION! Remove pan from heat and add brandy from measuring cup (never the bottle). IT WILL FLAME! Allow flames to die down.
3. Add garlic, remaining mustard, and beef stock. Bring to a boil, then lower heat to a simmer. Reduce liquid by half.
4. Stir in heavy cream. Bring to a simmer and cook for 2 minutes.
5. Stir in butter. Spoon over steak.

Shmetiquette

Scientists say the only thing that separates us from animals is our ability to reason. But what good is reason, when it is so easily lost in the presence of females and beer? If reason is truly the only thing keeping humans from walking on all fours, your dinner plans are in a lot of trouble.

Luckily, there's another distinguishing trait keeping us at the top of the evolutionary ladder—table manners. As fussy and frivolous as they may be, good table manners are a hallmark of acceptable behavior. Though the lexicon of etiquette is absurdly large, the following gems will help you get off on the right foot:

- *Master your napkin.* When sitting down to eat, place the napkin on your lap. When getting up from the table with the intent to return, place your napkin on the chair seat. When finished, place your napkin (unfolded) on the table.

- *Elbows off.* Sit up straight. Granted, this is the hardest work you've done in months, but it's a small price to pay.

- *Butter bread in pieces.* Never butter bread all at once. Break a bite-sized piece off, butter it, eat it, then tear another piece.

- *If she makes a faux pas, repeat it.* Show her that doing things her way is fine, even if it's poor etiquette. She uses the wrong fork? You use the wrong fork. She eats asparagus with her fingers? You eat asparagus with your fingers. She removes her top at the table? You get the idea.

Rack of Lamb with
Thyme-Mustard Coating

At no time during the evening should you speak of lambs in their non-chop form. Any mention of fluffy, white lambkins bouncing like popcorn across a meadow will at least make your date think twice about eating them, and at worst reduce her to tears. As far as you know, lamb chops are born, raised, and sold from the cool confines of the butcher case.

 DRINKS

With lamb's strong flavors, it's time to unleash the heavy hitters. A merlot or shiraz will have the bulk you need to match the strength of the sheep.

Wine seems your best bet, but if beer is a must, serve a dark lager such as German Dunkel.

 INGREDIENTS

The rack should come off a "spring lamb," which will have tender but flavorful meat. Do not use dried thyme or rosemary. Make the bread crumbs yourself by baking a few slices of sourdough in the oven (set to 200 degrees F) until dry (1–2 hours) and then crushing them in a food processor or in a Zip-loc bag with a rolling pin.

FOR THE COATING
1½ tablespoons olive oil
3 shallots, chopped
Salt and freshly ground black pepper
3 tablespoons balsamic vinegar

½ cup dried sourdough bread crumbs
1½ tablespoons chopped fresh thyme leaves
1 teaspoon fresh rosemary, chopped

FOR THE LAMB

1 rack of lamb, frenched (ask your butcher to do this) and trimmed of as much fat as possible

Salt and pepper to taste

1 tablespoon vegetable oil

1 teaspoon stone-ground mustard

Making the Coating

1. Place a skillet over medium heat. When hot, add oil and swirl to coat sides.
2. Add shallots, plus a pinch of salt and pepper. Stir frequently until shallots are golden brown (about 2 minutes). When they are brown, stir in vinegar. Cook until liquid is boiled off.
3. Remove from heat. Stir in bread crumbs, thyme, and rosemary. Set aside.

Roasting the Lamb

1. Place lamb on the counter long enough to bring it to room temperature (45 minutes or so).
2. Preheat oven to 400 degrees. Pat lamb dry, then season with salt and pepper.
3. Place a large frying pan over medium-high heat. When hot, add vegetable oil and swirl to coat sides.
4. Place lamb in pan and sear quickly on all sides until golden brown. Remove from pan and place in a roasting dish, rib side down.
5. Spread the mustard across the meat evenly, then press crumb mixture onto mustard. The meat should be evenly coated.
6. Place in the oven for 25 to 30 minutes, or until a meat thermometer reads 125 degrees F.
7. When done, remove from pan and place on a cutting board. Let sit for 8 minutes, then slice into chops.

Disaster Area

When the stove is off and the finishing touches are being applied to your meal, pause for a moment and assess the condition of your kitchen. Does it look like the aftermath of a cooking school student bender? Pots and pans everywhere? Ingredients and packaging strewn about the counters like tree limbs after a hurricane? If the answer is yes, then you're jeopardizing the success of your dinner.

Working in a cluttered, messy kitchen can have a decidedly negative impact on your final product. Your ability to control the elements is greatly reduced in a sloppy workspace, and things can easily spin out of control while you're knee deep in crap. Therefore, you should constantly remind yourself to employ the ancient technique of *CAYUGO,* or "clean as you go." Keep plenty of clean dish towels around for cleaning up spills. Work within reach of a garbage can and disposal, using both frequently. And, most important, return ingredients to the cupboards as soon as you are through with them. Your counters, and your head, should stay clear as a result, allowing you to focus on more important things.

Thai Cabbage Rolls with Peanut Sauce

With just about every color of the rainbow and every texture known to the palate, this Thai dish is one of the most visually appealing in the book. With little effort, you can create a meal that looks incredible and tastes even better. And when the food looks good, you look good. And when you look good . . .

 DRINKS

Again, Thai food provides you with the perfect excuse to suck down some malt liquor. Cold Singhas for everyone.

 INGREDIENTS

Napa cabbage is different from regular cabbage, and much better suited to this dish. Rice sticks are very thin noodles, sometimes called *mai fun* or glass noodles. Finally, make sure you don't confuse the hot sesame oil and the chili oil.

FOR THE ROLL SAUCE

½ cup soy sauce

¼ cup palm vinegar

2 tablespoons peanut oil

1 teaspoon hot sesame oil

1 teaspoon garlic, minced

½ teaspoon sugar

FOR THE PEANUT DIPPING SAUCE

2 tablespoons chopped garlic

½ cup chunky peanut butter

½ cup soy sauce

1 teaspoon sugar

1 tablespoon rice vinegar

1 tablespoon hot chili oil

FOR THE ROLLS

½ pound shrimp, shelled and deveined

1 head napa cabbage, leaves separated

½ cup carrots, julienne

½ red pepper, julienne

½ cup bean sprouts

½ cup cilantro leaves

½ cucumber, julienne

¼ cup green onion, julienne

1 handful mai fun, cooked according to package instructions

Making the Roll Sauce

1. Combine all ingredients in a small bowl. Stir, then set aside for later use.

Making the Peanut Sauce

1. Combine all ingredients in a bowl. Using a whisk, beat ingredients until smooth. Set aside for later use.

Making the Cabbage Rolls

1. Bring a pot of water to boil over high heat. Cook shrimp in boiling water. Remove just as shrimp begin to turn pink, about 2 minutes.
2. Arrange ingredients on counter. Place one cabbage leaf on a plate. Pile on ingredients as desired, then drizzle with soy-garlic sauce. Roll them up.
3. Go all out on presentation of the rolls. Serve with peanut sauce on the side (see below for a trick involving a squeeze bottle) and with rice as an accompaniment.

Presentation

It can taste and smell fantastic, but if it looks like crap she won't enjoy it. Therefore, spending a few seconds on presentation ("plating" as the pros call it) can make the difference between an okay meal and a memorable one. This doesn't mean you have to carve radishes into roses or make an Eiffel Tower out of the potatoes. Just spend a few seconds applying some of the following tricks of the trade.

- *Wipe the plate clean.* Sauce, broth, juices, etc. will tend to drip onto the outsides of a clean plate during serving. Right before putting the food on the table, wipe the edge clean with a towel.

- *Garnish.* If the dish features an herb in the ingredients, place a fresh sprig of the same alongside the food. Same goes with tomato slices, fruit wedges, etc.

- *Squeeze bottle.* To get the Jackson Pollock look on the sauce application, use a ketchup squeeze bottle.

- *Use odd numbers.* Five or seven pieces of asparagus, not six or eight. One or three medallions of beef, not two or four.

New York Steak with Horseradish Gorgonzola Sauce and Rice Pilaf

This recipe brings us to the topic of the after-dinner mint. The combination of Gorgonzola cheese and horseradish will not leave you smelling like a fresh mountain breeze—a problem when the evening's activities take a turn toward the intimate. You could reach for a pack of gum or a roll of Certs, but doing so will tip her to your imminent plan for mashing face. Instead, serve a small bowl of vanilla ice cream garnished with a fresh sprig of mint for dessert. The vanilla will neutralize the harshest odors, while the mint functions as a natural freshener, leaving you to operate confidently in close quarters.

 DRINKS

Traditionally, red meat likes red wine. If you're feeling like bucking the trend a bit, serve the same dry chardonnay that you use in the sauce.

The sharp flavors of horseradish will need an equally sharp beverage, and a highly hopped Pale Ale should do the trick.

 INGREDIENTS

New York steak, the next-door neighbor of filet mignon, is a subtly flavored option that the females might prefer. Any cut of meat, however, will work with this sauce. Remember to buy prepared horseradish, but not a horseradish "cream" that contains additional ingredients.

FOR THE PILAF

½ stick of butter

1 cup short grain rice

½ cup vermicelli, crushed into ½-inch-long pieces

Salt to taste

2 cups canned low-sodium chicken broth

FOR THE SAUCE
1 tablespoon butter
2 shallots, chopped
¼ cup chardonnay
1 cup heavy cream
1 cup Gorgonzola cheese, crumbled
¼ cup plus 1 tablespoon prepared horseradish
½ teaspoon salt
½ teaspoon freshly ground black pepper
1 tablespoon flat-leaf parsley, chopped

FOR THE STEAK
2 8-ounce New York steaks, preferably dry-aged
   Salt and freshly ground black pepper to taste

 ## Making the Pilaf

1. Place a saucepan over medium-high heat. Add butter to pan and melt.

2. When butter is melted, add rice, vermicelli, and salt. Sauté, stirring constantly until golden brown.

3. When browning is complete, add chicken broth and stir. Bring mixture to a boil, then cover and reduce heat to a simmer until liquid is absorbed.

4. Taste rice for doneness. Add more broth and continue to simmer if underdone. Keep warm in oven (175 degrees F) until ready to serve.

Making the Sauce

1. Place a small saucepan over medium heat. Place butter in pan. When butter is melted and bubbling, add shallots. Sauté until translucent, about 4 minutes.

2. Add wine. Cook until wine is almost entirely reduced, about 3 minutes.

3. Add cream. Bring to a boil, then reduce heat and simmer for 90 seconds.

4. Using a whisk, add Gorgonzola and horseradish, one spoonful at a time. Whisk in completely, then add the next spoonful.

5. When cheese and horseradish are completely blended in, add salt and pepper. Remove from heat and whisk in parsley. Set aside and move on to next stage.

Searing the Steaks

1. Preheat oven to 400 degrees F. Pat steaks dry and season all surfaces with salt and pepper.
2. Place a heavy, ovenproof skillet over high heat. Wait for pan to become very hot.
3. Sear first side of steak until brown, about 4 minutes. On second side, sear for one minute. Place pan directly in oven and roast until medium-rare (about 7 minutes, depending on thickness).

Serving

1. Drizzle sauce over steak and serve alongside pilaf.

Well Done

"Just be yourself" is solid dating advice . . . unless, of course, your self wants his steak well done. In that case, tell him to grow up and eat beef like a gentleman should: medium-rare.

Cooking the you-know-what out of a steak will render even the tastiest cut of meat useless. A well-done, dry New York steak will taste about the same as a well-done, dry chunk of horsemeat (the latter saving you about 23 dollars on the pound). With the flavorful juices and fats effectively cooked off, a well-done steak is little more than a fleshy workout for your back teeth. Properly cooked steak, on the other hand, is a thing of beauty—tender, juicy, and literally bursting with flavor.

As discussed earlier in the book, the food we eat can serve as a reliable credential check. Unfortunately, a preference for well-done steak, no matter how innocent, is liable to sabotage any attempts at respectability. What will you do for an encore? Dip it in ranch dressing? Sprinkle crushed Doritos on top? If you can't eat it medium-rare, save your steak-eating forays for trips to Sizzler.

Angel Hair Pasta with Garlic and Peas

Girls stop by your house about as often as a direct strike of lightning. When it does happen, however, you need to be prepared to offer them something to eat other than reheated pizza. Speed is of the essence. The ingredients must be on hand, and the meal has to be ready to go before she catches wind of your ruse. With haste . . .

 DRINKS

If you have one wine on hand at all times, make it chardonnay. Most people, if not all, will drink it and be satisfied.

Likewise, a golden lager-style beer will be pleasantly neutral.

 INGREDIENTS

The peas can be frozen and the pasta can be dried. The real key will be to use the highest quality olive oil you can get your hands on.

2 tablespoons olive oil	1 cup cooked peas
2 tablespoons plus 1 teaspoon minced garlic	Salt and freshly ground black pepper
1 pound angel hair pasta	

Making the Sauce

1. Place a small skillet over medium heat. When pan is hot, add oil, swirling to coat sides.
2. Add garlic to pan and cook until golden brown.

Boiling the Pasta

1. Follow the directions on the package for al dente pasta, and cook it for 30 seconds fewer than indicated.
2. Drain pasta and return to pot.
3. Pour oil and garlic into pot and toss with pasta. Turn on heat to low, and stir in peas. Warm the mixture through, season with salt and pepper, and serve.

Location, Location, Location

We'd all like to know where, exactly, the characters in porn flicks live. What neighborhood is this, where beautiful women are constantly stopping by, knocking on the door, needing to come in for some reason or another? They stop by to borrow sugar, and end up staying for sex. They ask to use the phone, and hang out to use the shower. They return your lost puppy, and end up wearing the collar. If you discover this neighborhood, buy a house there . . . and never leave home.

It's not that women never stop by your place, it's just that when they do, the Vegas odds of you having sex with them are effectively zero. Imagine, though, that at a moment's notice you could offer a girl a delicious home-cooked meal and a glass of wine, all in about 20 minutes. By keeping the ingredients you need on hand at all times, you can fire off a dinner invite at a moment's notice. Maybe then you can improve your drop-by success-to-failure ratio, without investing in speculative, fantasyland real estate.

Venison with Red Wine Sauce and Pears

God bless you if you can successfully slay and clean a deer. God bless you twice if you know a girl that would actually join you for the eating of said deer.

Whether you go the James Fenimore Cooper route or simply pick up some game at the gourmet grocery store, you have to resist the manly urge to eat venison raw with your hands. Even though your food may have recently been strapped to a car hood, you should always display proper etiquette (see box on p. 91). Who knows, she may appreciate a subtle blend of wildman and sophisticate, and you'll have the chance to bag a doe to match your buck.

 DRINKS

Venison boasts strong flavors, so break out a whopping red, say cabernet sauvignon.

"Old Milwaukee goes perfect with deer!" Yes, but if you're eating in a wheel-less home, reach for a dark, micro-brewed lager. It should have the complexity and body to match the venison.

 INGREDIENTS

A good many grocery stores carry venison these days, but if you can't find it, use a substitute. Elk, wild boar, ostrich, and even grass-fed beef will suffice.

FOR THE SAUCE

2 cups red wine

1 shallot, chopped

½ cup cooked carrots, pureed with a food processor

Salt and pepper

⅔ cup chilled butter, cut into small pats

FOR THE VENISON

6 medallions (noisettes) of venison

3 tablespoons butter (for making 2 tablespoons clarified butter)

FOR THE PEARS

4 peeled and cored pears, halved and sliced thin

2 tablespoons butter

Clarifying the Butter

1. Place butter in a saucepan. Place pan over low heat and let the butter melt slowly. Do not stir.

2. As the butter melts, a layer of foam will form on top. Using a spoon, carefully remove foam.

3. Of the two layers left, you want the top one. Pour off the clear yellow liquid into a separate bowl. This is your clarified butter.

Starting the Sauce

1. Bring red wine to a boil long enough to evaporate alcohol, about 2 minutes.

2. Add chopped shallot. Lower heat, keeping pan at a simmer until liquid is reduced by half.

3. Add pureed carrots, salt, and pepper. Stir to blend evenly and remove from heat. Set aside.

Browning the Pears

1. Spread slices of pears into fans that can be flipped with a spatula (cook the pears in batches if it would be easier).

2. Heat a frying pan over medium heat. Add butter.

3. When butter is melted, add pears. Cook fans of pears on each side until lightly browned, about 2 minutes.

Frying the Venison

1. Place a skillet over high heat. Place clarified butter in pan.
2. When butter is melted, add venison and cook for about 2 minutes on each side, or until outside is browned and interior is only slightly pink. Remove venison and place on paper towels to drain.
3. Add 3 tablespoons of water. Scrape the bottom of the pan with a spatula to release venison flavors (a technique called deglazing). When bottom is clean, remove from heat. Set liquid aside for addition to the sauce.

Finishing the Sauce

1. Reheat sauce over medium heat. Whisking vigorously, blend in pats of butter one at a time.
2. Add liquid from venison pan and stir.

Serving

Spoon a thin layer of sauce onto a plate. Place fanned pears and venison side by side in the sauce.

Zig Zag

In Turkey, etiquette demands that you use only your right hand to eat. This is a tradition born of necessity, as the left hand is reserved for a far less pleasant task. Here in America, our etiquette has less to do with hygiene and more to do with making a favorable impression (i.e., getting laid).

Regardless of how you choose to get food into your mouth when dining alone, in the company of a fair female you should employ the "Zig Zag method." Named and formalized by etiquette guru Emily Post, the method is designed to enforce a slow, methodic pace of eating—a good thing when the focus of your evening is food, conversation, and quality time. The following guidelines should get you off on the right foot:

- *Only the right . . . or only the left.* Utensils should only be brought to the mouth with your dominant hand. If you have difficulty remembering, just pretend your weak hand is Turkish.

- *One cut, one bite.* When eating food that must be cut with a knife (steak, for instance), hold the fork in your weak hand with the tines pointing downward. Then, use your dominant hand to cut a small bite-sized piece of the food. Finally, switch hands and use the fork to place the single bite in your mouth. Repeat.

- *Once used, don't replace.* After you use a particular piece of silverware, never place it back on the tablecloth. Instead, rest it on your plate.

- *Finished.* When done, place your silverware on your plate parallel to each other and at the 2 o'clock position, with the handles to your right. This signifies to your date that you are done and ready to move on. If she doesn't get the hint, a gentle rustling of the condom wrapper in your pocket should suffice.

Cooking for All Occasions

The prototypical chick-magnet meal involves an invitation to dinner on your home turf, a well-planned, well-prepared meal, and a reaping of the rewards you have so carefully sown. The kitchen, dining room, and bedroom are all familiar. The home-field advantage is yours, and you're looking to sweep the series.

But opportunities for impressing chicks with food abound, and to get at them we sometimes need to take our show on the road. It may require some extra planning or a little finagling, but since your desire doesn't get checked on your way out the front door, why should your skills? In the following pages, we'll address some classic scenarios and situations in which we can cook for chicks outside the comfy environs of home.

Trout Foil Packets with Garlic Bread

Cooking for a Camping Trip

Women love it when men tame the elements, and here's your big chance. She won't care that the road to the campsite was paved, the shower takes quarters, or that the lesbian at the ranger station is one cry of "Help!" away. All she'll notice is that even out in the great wilderness, you're able to provide a great meal.

To that end, foil packets are a camper's best friend. They go right in the coals and produce a frying/steaming effect that leaves fish incredibly moist and flavorful. Use this recipe and the tips that follow to make sure you experience the joy of joys that is "tent sex."

 DRINKS

In the interest of light packing and convenience, you can't argue with finishing off the chardonnay required for the recipe.

 INGREDIENTS

To keep the packing to a minimum, the ingredients are as simple as can be. Also, this recipe assumes that you can catch a trout on your camping trip—in other words, have a backup plan.

FOR THE GARLIC BREAD
- 1 small loaf of french bread
- 3 tablespoons butter, softened
- 2 garlic cloves, minced

FOR THE TROUT PACKET
- 1 or 2 whole trout (enough for two)
- Salt and pepper

- 2 tablespoons butter
- 1 shallot, chopped
- 1 garlic clove, chopped
- 1 small bunch thyme
- 4 slices orange
- 2 slices lemon
- ¼ cup chardonnay

Making the Garlic Bread

1. Make slices (½ inch apart) in the loaf, not quite through to the bottom.
2. Combine garlic and butter. Spread mixture evenly on each slice.
3. Place bread on large piece of foil. Fold ends and seal.

Making the Trout Packets

1. Wait until the campfire is reduced to glowing embers over which you can grill.
2. Lay trout on large piece of aluminum foil. Add salt and pepper to taste.
3. Open trout and insert butter, half of shallot and garlic.
4. Insert half of the thyme sprigs into the trout, and lay remaining half on top. Scatter remaining shallot and garlic on top as well.
5. Lay the fruit wedges on top of the trout, and pour chardonnay over all. Seal packet by folding foil width-wise, then making multiple folds on the ends.

Grilling the Packets

1. Choose an area of moderately hot coals in which to place the packet.
2. Place both the bread and fish packets on embers. Cook for about 15 minutes, flipping the fish packets once halfway through.
3. Remove packets and check. Bread is done when toasted on the outside. Fish is done when moist and flaky. Continue to cook if desired doneness is not reached.
4. Serve on plates, or eat directly off the foil.

Tent Sex

To ensure tent sex, Ranger Rick, follow these camping and cooking tips:

- *Double-check your ingredient list.* The store is a long ways away, and it would be a shame if your meal gets ruined because you forgot the salt.

- *Stay dry.* Use ice packs instead of ice to keep food cold. Any trace of water in the food can ruin a meal.

- *Start in daylight.* Cooking will get increasingly more difficult as the sun goes down. By the time the sun sets, the after-dinner cocoa and sleeping bag footsy should be well under way.

- *Mind the fire.* In her eyes, the only thing worse than failure to build a solid campfire is failure to get your tent-pole up.

Brown Sugar Glazed Ham

Cooking for a Potluck

When your boss's doe-eyed niece asks, "What did *you* bring?" you'll want to have something to say other than, "Chips, just chips." With this perfect potluck recipe (great warm, great cold), you'll be able to look her square in the eyes and say, "I brought the large piece of meat that everyone's talking about. Would you like some?"

 DRINKS

Should be taken care of by the hosts. If not, the "let's ditch this place and go get a drink" pickup line should be used freely.

 INGREDIENTS

You can get an acceptable cured ham for around $1.75 per pound. Everything else is fairly straightforward.

FOR THE HAM

- 1 (10- to 13-pound) skinless, shankless, cured ham, smoked
- ½ cup whole cloves

FOR THE GLAZE

- 1 cup packed light brown sugar
- ¼ cup plus 1 tablespoon Dijon mustard
- 2 tablespoons cider vinegar

Preparing the Ham for Roasting

1. Preheat the oven to 350 degrees F. Score the top of the ham by making shallow cuts with a sharp knife. After scoring, the top of the ham should be covered with small ½-inch diamonds.
2. Place a whole clove in each of the crosses in the scoring.

Roasting the Ham

1. Place ham in a large roasting pan, and roast for 1½ hours.
2. Remove from oven for glazing.

Glazing and Finishing

1. Combine glaze ingredients in a bowl.
2. Spread glaze evenly over entire ham.
3. Return ham to oven and roast for 35 minutes.
4. Remove ham and let cool for fifteen minutes before serving. Can be served warm or cold. At the potluck, place a sharp knife on the serving plate and let people cut their own pieces.

Potluck

The dictionary defines *potluck* as "the chance that whatever is available will prove to be good or acceptable." Considering the flurry of Jell-O desserts, mystery casseroles, and dodgy bean dips that continue to feature in the potluck tradition, the Vegas odds on "good or acceptable" appear to be extraordinarily long. Indeed, most of what you find at your local "last-names-beginning-with-A-through-D-bring-a-salad" dinner party can be more appropriately described as "shit luck."

To break from the norm, find a good recipe (like the previous one) that travels well and tastes just as good at room temperature as it does piping hot from the oven. Skip any foodstuffs that will wither or lose color over time such as spinach, apples, or avocado. And, most important, don't be one of those potluck-chumps who pony up a 12-piece bucket of Original Recipe. The Colonel may have been a Southern belle slayer in his day, but he's of no use to you now.

Roast Beef with Sour Cream
Horseradish Spread

Cooking for a Picnic

The scene that probably comes to mind is the ubiquitous "picnic in the park," perfect if you like to be interrupted by slobbering retrievers, soon-to-be-missing children, and stray soccer balls from the UN-sponsored pick-up game. Not exactly a scene dripping with erotic potential.

Instead, head for a place where the crowds are relatively low to nonexistent. An early spring beach trip would be perfect, as would a weekday jaunt to the nearest state park. Closer to home, a city rooftop meal can make for the perfect blend of convenience and solitude. In all, just run down a list of where, all things being equal, a girl would most likely agree to get nude outdoors.

 DRINKS

On a hot summer's day, a chilled chardonnay will be a nice thirst-quencher. The beef, though, opens the door for a red, say, pinot noir.

Lugging multiple bottles of beer around can be a hassle. Instead, grab a 24-ounce bottle of Heineken and two glasses.

 INGREDIENTS

Set the beef out on the counter for an hour before roasting. This will bring the meat to room temperature, allowing for more even doneness. Roast the meat the day before, then leave it in the fridge overnight.

FOR THE ROAST BEEF

1 tablespoon dried peppercorns, ground

1 teaspoon dried green peppercorns, ground

1 teaspoon white peppercorns, ground

1 teaspoon coarse salt

1 3-pound fillet of beef, trimmed

FOR THE SAUCE

1 cup sour cream

3 teaspoons horseradish

Salt and freshly ground black pepper

Pinch of paprika

Roasting the Fillet

1. Preheat oven to 500 degrees F. Combine the dry ingredients in a small mixing bowl.
2. Rub fillet with mixture until the meat is evenly coated.
3. Place a large skillet over high heat. When hot, sear beef on all sides until brown.
4. Place fillet in an oiled roasting pan, then place in oven. Roast until a meat thermometer (inserted into the center of the fillet) reads approximately 125 degrees F. This should take around 20 minutes.
5. Remove from oven, let cool, then refrigerate.

Making the Sauce and Serving

1. Before picnic, mix sauce ingredients in a sealable container. Adjust ingredients until desired flavor is reached.
2. Cut roast into thin slices. Serve with fresh bread, vegetables, and the sauce.

Chicken Soup

Cooking for Her When She's Sick

Her throat hurts, her nose is stuffed, her head throbs . . . and your ears ache from hearing about it. It's a grueling task, yes, but by providing food in her time of need, you're amassing some serious points that can be redeemed in the future. She'll remember your good deeds and thank you properly in good time. Cook her this chicken soup at your house and deliver it in the pot to get her on the road to recovery.

 DRINKS

Probably none for her, but feel free to sauce yourself up with the drink of your choice. It will make playing nurse much more tolerable. If she's coughing, a little nip of brandy might help suppress it.

 INGREDIENTS

To avoid the blandness typical of most chicken soups, use a kosher chicken. Having been brined (soaked in saltwater), a kosher chicken will provide a richer, more complex flavor.

FOR THE STOCK
1   kosher chicken, quartered
    and rinsed
    Salt and freshly ground black
    pepper
2   tablespoons extra virgin olive
    oil

1   large, sweet onion, chopped
2   stalks celery, sliced
3   carrots, sliced
6   cups water

FOR FINISHING
¼   cup chopped parsley
1   cup small egg noodles

Making the Stock

1. Rinse, pat dry, and season the chicken pieces liberally with salt and pepper.
2. Heat a heavy-bottomed stockpot on medium-high. When hot, add oil and swirl to coat sides.
3. Add onion and celery. Cook, stirring occasionally, until translucent.
4. Using a spatula, clear a place in the pan for the chicken. Place chicken in pan, skin side down, and brown for 5 minutes.
5. Add carrots and water. Bring to a boil, then reduce heat and simmer for 1 hour.

Finishing

1. Remove chicken from soup. When chicken is cool enough to be handled, strip meat from bones. Return meat to the soup and discard the waste.
2. Stir in parsley and egg noodles. Cook for another 8 minutes. Serve with saltine crackers or warm bread.

Caprese Sandwich with Homemade Potato Chips

Cooking for the Brown Bag Lunch

There are all sorts of situations that call for a sack lunch: a field trip to the museum, a hike to the nearest waterfall, even an extended work lunch in the park. Inviting her is a great idea, but packing her a soggy, deformed PB&J with a side of dry, cracked carrot sticks is not. Turn your sack lunch into a sex lunch with the following recipe.

A close relative of the salad by the same name, the Caprese sandwich is perfect for lunch. By the time noon rolls around, the olive oil and balsamic vinegar will have soaked the sourdough to perfection, leaving a wonderfully flavored and textured sandwich. Homemade chips complete the equation.

 DRINKS

The key to a great sack lunch is simplicity, and working drinks into the equation can be tough. Then again, you gotta have booze. Pack a half bottle of chardonnay along with two plastic, collapsible glasses.

 INGREDIENTS

All the same recommendations that apply to the salad apply to the sandwich. Use the finest olive oil, vinegar, and tomatoes you can. Buffalo mozzarella is, obviously, made from buffalo milk, and should be purchased fresh (i.e., packed in water). Arugula is a leafy green with a slight hint of pepper flavor. If you can't find it, a few sprigs of basil will substitute.

FOR THE POTATO CHIPS

2 pounds Russet (baking) potatoes, sliced 1/16-inch thick

Peanut oil for frying

Salt to taste

FOR THE SANDWICH

2 tomatoes, sliced

2 tablespoons olive oil

½ small red onion, sliced very thin

2 tablepoons balsamic vinegar

2 sourdough sandwich rolls or 1 sourdough baguette cut into 2 sandwich portions

Freshly ground black pepper and salt to taste

¼-inch slices of fresh buffalo mozzarella, enough to layer sandwich

1 cup arugula leaves

Frying the Potato Chips

1. Soak potato slices in lukewarm water for 30 minutes. Drain and dry with a spinner before frying. Pat dry with paper towels. *Any water will cause oil to pop and splatter!*

2. Place a heavy-bottomed stockpot over high heat. Fill pot to 2 inches depth with oil (should be no more than ⅓ full). Using a thermometer, heat oil to around 355 degrees F.

3. In small batches, add potatoes to oil and fry until golden brown (around 2 minutes per batch).

4. Remove chips from oil with a slotted spoon. Set to drain on paper towels.

5. When thermometer again reaches 355, fry the next batch. Repeat until all potatoes are fried.

6. Sprinkle with salt while still hot.

Making the Sandwich

1. In a bowl, combine tomatoes, olive oil, red onion and balsamic vinegar. Toss tomatoes to coat.

2. Slice bread. Using a brush, lightly coat open faces with oil and vinegar from the tomato mixture.

3. Layer bread with mozzarella, tomato, and onion. Add arugula, salt, and pepper and close sandwich. Wrap in tin foil and refrigerate (would also be fine for a few hours unrefrigerated in a paper bag).

Cooler Chili

Cooking for a Tailgate

The institution that is tailgating forms a continuum between two clearly divided poles. On one end of the spectrum sit alumni boosters clad in lettermen's sweaters, sipping white wine and enjoying crackers with olive tapanade. The other pole is home to beer-helmet and face-paint-wearing, high-five-slapping types munching Doritos and funneling Milwaukee's Best. The only thing the two scenes have in common is a complete dearth of females.

Somewhere in between there's a tailgate party that can provide the setting for an epic afternoon of womanizing. As the beer flows and the food is dished out in heaps, you can count on missing the first quarter to chat up some bird . . . and ditching the fourth so you can rush her home for overtime. But you'll need food. Read on.

 DRINKS

Wine probably isn't the best call here, unless you're willing to endure the clowning of your buddies (it's a tailgate, for chrissake). If you must, drinking it straight from the bottle might lessen the heckling.

As long as the beer's cold, it's good enough to drink.

 INGREDIENTS

Nothing fancy here, just hearty standards. The only trick is getting it to the game. To pull it off, wash out an appropriately sized cooler with hot soapy water. Rinse thoroughly with scalding water, then load the chili right there.

2 tablespoons olive oil

1½ cups onions, chopped

8 large garlic cloves, chopped

2 shallots, chopped

3 pounds ground sirloin

1 28-ounce can crushed tomatoes

1 6-ounce can tomato paste

1 12-ounce bottle Newcastle Brown Ale

14½-ounces canned low-sodium chicken broth

5 tablespoons chili powder

½ teaspoon dried oregano

½ teaspoon dried thyme

1 tablespoon plus 1 teaspoon ground cumin

1 teaspoon dried basil

¼ teaspoon marjoram

1 15- to 16-ounce can prepared pinto beans

Salt and pepper

Sautéing

1. Heat a large, heavy stockpot or Dutch oven over medium heat. When hot, add oil, swirling to coat bottom.
2. Add onions, shallots, and garlic to pot. Sauté, stirring occasionally, until onions are translucent.
3. Add ground beef, stirring to break up meat. Cook until brown (about 5 minutes). Move immediately to next stage.

Simmering

1. Add tomatoes, paste, beer, and broth. Add dry ingredients and stir until mixed evenly. Bring mixture to a boil, then lower heat to a simmer.
2. Simmer, stirring occasionally, for about 1 hour and 15 minutes. Then mix in chili beans. Simmer for 5 more minutes. Taste, and season with salt and pepper as needed.

Transferring

Pour chili straight from pot into cooler and seal lid until serving. The chili has to go in hot, otherwise it won't stay hot (and if it doesn't, bacteria will start to hump in it).

◆ Grilling ◆

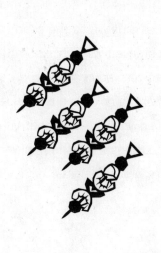

When meat is to be cooked over flame, with only God's sky above, women climb into the backseat. Men take the culinary helm, steering the ship out of the calm waters of domesticity and into the stormy seas of canned beer and overdone steak. For an afternoon, food belongs to us, and we'll do with it as we damn well please.

But there's an alternative to the road of hot dogs and blatant intoxication, and it's paved with chicks. In the pages that follow, we'll discuss how to turn your grill into a sophisticated, female-charming beast. With simple, casual recipes designed for a laid-back afternoon affair, you'll have all that you need to move this cooking-for-chicks business into the backyard. Grab the tongs and matches, we're grillin' for girls.

Carne Asada

The direct translation is "roast meat," but this dish is much more than that. Good in tacos, burritos, or by itself with a side of beans and rice, this traditional Mexican preparation produces tender, flavorful beef that is sure to satisfy any carnivorous chick. After the meal, blindfold her, and let her whack away at your piñata.

 DRINKS

The red meat, with peppery, citrus flavors will be complemented nicely by a zinfandel.

For beer, go with the slightly darker (by Mexican-beer standards) Negra Modelo.

 INGREDIENTS

Typically, skirt steak is best for carne asada, but any thinly sliced beef will work. Fresh lime juice means juice from an actual lime, not a green plastic lime with a yellow cap.

1 pound skirt steak, sliced very thin	Seasoned pepper
Juice from 2 limes	Salt

Marinating the Steak

1. Lay thin slices of meat in a shallow dish. Season both sides of meat liberally with salt and pepper.
2. Pour lime juice over all and let sit for one hour before grilling.

Searing the Carne Asada

1. Bring barbeque to an intense heat. When heat is as high as it will go, quickly sear both sides of the meat. Remove as soon as grill marks are made (if fire is hot, cook for no more than about 2 minutes on each side for medium-rare).
2. Serve with beans, rice, and warm tortillas.

Why Barbequing Works: Take 1

Before the advent of BMWs and Prada shoes, women evaluated a man's "sex-worthiness" according to his ability to secure basic necessities. Those that provided the steaks got the thanks. Food was hard to come by, and the act of procuring it took up the majority of early man's time. Roots and berries were a nice find, but the real score came in the form of—God bless it—meat, which was high in energy and loaded with protein. Coming back to camp with a large mammal slung over your shoulder meant you'd live to hunt another day. It also meant you'd have your pick of the cave-chick litter.

After hundreds of thousands of years, that evolutionarily sound arrangement became hard-wired into the female mind. Today, when you step behind the grill to cook a thick piece of meat over raw flame, you're tapping in to those very strong associations. Provide the meat, and you might just get thanked for it.

Chicken Malay

The moment when you first see her without makeup can be a trying one. Who knows what she's been hiding under those carefully applied layers of foundation, mascara, and eye shadow? Occasionally, you'll find a girl who, when stripped of chemical assistance, doesn't look like her long-lost, pale, ugly twin. And when you do, hold on to her.

So it goes with Chicken Malay. On any other night, you may recognize the distinct flavors of this dish going by another name— Tandoori Chicken. This version, however, skips the obnoxious red food dye that accompanies most Tandoori dishes, and opts for a more simple, traditional Malaysian preparation.

 DRINKS

Indian-style foods, with their bold flavors and aromas, can be a challenge for some wines. A chardonnay that leans toward the fruity side will hold its own.

Any excuse to consume beer that comes in liter-sized bottles should be jumped at. The Indian classics Taj Mahal and Kingfisher are both sold in the large bottles, and both taste great with this dish.

 INGREDIENTS

The spices that form the basis of Malaysian food are becoming increasingly common at your local supermarket. If you look and can't find, order the spices off the internet a few weeks in advance (see Resource Guide, page 165)—one bottle will be as good as a lifetime supply.

FOR THE MARINADE

½ cup plain yogurt

2 tablespoons buttermilk

2 teaspoons chili garlic sauce

1 tablespoon soy sauce

1 tablespoon minced ginger

¼ cup cilantro leaves

1 tablespoon green onion, chopped

2 teaspoons sugar

¼ teaspoon cardamom

½ teaspoon turmeric

½ teaspoon coriander

¼ teaspoon pepper

Pinch of salt

FOR THE CHICKEN

4 thighs and 4 legs, separated

Cooking oil

FOR THE BREAD

2 pieces white pita bread

3 tablespoons olive oil

2 cloves garlic, minced

Marinating the Chicken

1. In a large bowl, combine marinade ingredients and stir.
2. Add chicken and toss to coat. Cover with foil and place in refrigerator for 12 to 18 hours.

Making the Bread

1. Preheat oven to 350 degrees F. In a small bowl, combine garlic and olive oil. Let sit for 10 minutes to allow garlic to infuse oil.
2. Brush top of pita with the garlic oil. Place on a baking sheet and bake until top is golden, about 5 minutes.

Grilling the Chicken

1. Bring fire to high heat.
2. Remove chicken from marinade with a slotted spoon. Before placing on grill, lightly brush chicken with cooking oil, then brush grill as well.
3. Cook on grill (3 inches above coals) until meat is no longer pink, about 25 to 30 minutes.

Why Barbequing Works: Take 2

The wood's wet, the lighter fluid is almost gone, and the ten matches you started with have dwindled down to two. Her suspicious gaze is burning a hole right through you, and you know what she's thinking: "What kind of asshole doesn't know how to build a fire?"

Women want to feel safe and secure, and to them a man who can't build a fire might as well be a eunuch. If you can skillfully and successfully manage your grill, however, you're proving to her that fire is your friend. Whether the grill uses charcoal or gas is beside the point. Manipulating a flame shows you're in command of the elements. If you had to cook freshly caught trout in the woods, you could, and searing filet mignon on the back porch is no problem, either. For women, a man in control of his fire is appealing, and that can make the difference between a cold shoulder and a flaming-hot end to the evening.

Grilled Dungeness Crab
with Basil Butter

Though crabs are one of the few foodstuffs you can still purchase live, don't. The eerie clacking of shell against steel that would result from a Dungeness' futile attempts to escape your closed grill would be more than your date could handle. Remember, when cooking for a chick, anything that calls to mind feelings of entrapment and a need for escape should be avoided at all costs.

 DRINKS

Butter and crab are great wine fare. Serve a creamy chardonnay or an oaky sauvignon blanc, and you'll be chasing every bite.

Oregon is famous for its Dungeness and, increasingly, for its ale. Grab a micro-brewed pale to go with this dish.

 INGREDIENTS

The crab should be a brilliant orange to red in color. If it's brown and dull, it probably isn't too good. Use fresh basil, not dried.

FOR THE BUTTER

- ½ pound butter
- 1 garlic clove, minced
- ¼ cup chopped basil
- Fresh ground pepper to taste

FOR THE CRAB

- 2 Dungeness crabs, cooked and cleaned (you can have your fishmonger do this)

Making the Butter

1. Find a spot on the barbeque that approximates a medium-low heat (move coals to one side and place crab opposite). Place a saucepan directly on the grill over that spot. Add butter, garlic, pepper, and basil to pan.
2. Melt butter and stir ingredients. Keep warm until next step, but do not allow butter to brown.

Grilling the Crab

1. Crab should be cooked and cleaned. Place the crabs on aluminum foil. Bring edges of foil up around crabs. Leave top open, but ensure that sides are high enough to hold liquid.
2. Place crab and foil on grill. Pour butter mixture into the foil, taking care to cover each crab.
3. Cook for about 12 minutes, or until crabs are hot. Baste throughout the cooking time.
4. Remove crabs from grill. Serve with butter drained from the foil. Accompany with warm French bread.

Why Barbequing Works: Take 3

Think back to what you know (little, we hope) about male strippers. More specifically, focus on the uniforms most commonly worn by these entertainers. Typical images might include a cowboy outfit, possibly a policeman's uniform and, certainly, construction workers' garb. You'll notice that few strippers choose to assume the character of "Stephen the CPA" or "Phillip the Pediatrician." Instead, personas with limited educations, callused hands, and dubious grammar skills get the nod . . . and the women go crazy.

The costume themes employed by male revues tap into a common female fantasy; manual laborers and rugged types know how to please a woman in bed. Similarly, the very act of cooking meat over fire is a rugged, manly concept. When you saddle up behind the grill, work the tongs like an expert, and handle your meat like it was your job, she'll be entertaining the notion that you're the manly man she's been looking for. Hard hat and leather thong aside, the barbeque is a great accessory when it comes to flexing your manhood.

The Bacon Cheeseburger

Sometimes, girls like to go slumming. They'll forsake their normal standards (well dressed, polite manner, healthy stock portfolio) and head off to bed with an unshaven, motorcycle-riding lout, leaving you to wonder if there is any justice in the world.

It's the same with food. The very girl that reads labels, counts preservatives, and only drinks soy milk that comes from organic beans will occasionally see fit to sink her teeth into some serious junk food. When the mood strikes her, she wants to eat something that she'll regret. Enter the bacon cheeseburger. The daintiest, prissiest girl you know will attack this sandwich with guiltless abandon, knowing full well that she'll regret it the next day. Hopefully, for your sake, this will get the ball rolling and she'll follow one regrettable action with another.

 DRINKS

Dress up the evening with a bottle of cabernet sauvignon. The rich flavor of ground beef and the sharpness of the cheese will complement the wine well.

Of course, burgers are beer food, and pretty much any beer will work. A light Pilsner such as Pilsner Urquell would be particularly nice.

 INGREDIENTS

There's a high degree of flexibility here, so let personal preference guide you. However, that doesn't mean breaking out the yellow mustard squeeze bottle. Use high-quality ingredients to elevate your version of the bacon burger.

FOR THE PATTY

¾ pound ground chuck
   Garlic salt and pepper to
   taste
1 tablespoon fresh lemon juice
1 tablespoon soy sauce
2 slices bacon, fried in a skillet
   until crisp

FOR THE SANDWICH

¼ cup grated, extra sharp,
   white cheddar cheese
2 leaves romaine lettuce
2 slices fresh tomato
1 Cuban or Portuguese roll (or
   any available crusty, white
   roll)
   Desired condiments

Making the Patty

1. Prepare grill to high heat. Shape meat into two square-shaped patties. Handle meat as little as possible to avoid toughening.
2. Season with garlic salt and pepper.

Grilling the Patty

1. Mix soy sauce and lemon juice together in a small bowl.
2. Place patty on hot grill. When first side is done, flip burger and pour half of soy-lemon mixture over each patty. Add grated cheese to top of each patty.
3. Cook until desired doneness is reached and cheese is melted. When patties are almost done, throw rolls on the grill to toast.
4. Stack patties and ingredients on the rolls and serve with desired accompaniments.

The Fuel Debate: Gas

For as long as there have been barbeques, men have been debating about which fuel, gas or charcoal, produces the best grilling results. In truth, every minute spent arguing over this quandary is a minute wasted. Both fuels have their advantages. In the first of two installments, we'll look at the case for gas-fueled grills.

The Case for Gas: Convenience is a powerful thing. It keeps 7-Eleven in business, drives the technology industry, and causes thousands of men to continue to date moderately annoying women in exchange for readily available sex . . . no small feat.

In the world of grilling, convenience means gas. Push-button lighting, heat control with the turn of a knob, and maintenance that demands little more than a moist towel makes grilling with gas the epitome of ease. Never will the food taste like its been marinated in lighter fluid. Absent are the soot marks on the khakis. No waiting for the fire to heat up, and no waiting for the ashes to cool down. As simple as a stove outdoors, gas takes a lot of the hassle out of grilling, leaving you to focus on more important matters.

Boddingtons Chicken

This recipe is a novelty act, and goes over best after you and your date have knocked back a few beers. Set it up as if the idea just occurred to you. If she's the right girl, in the right frame of mind, she'll be impressed by your resourcefulness and creativity—quite a feat considering you suffer from a huge shortage of both.

 DRINKS

You've just stuffed a beer can up a chicken's ass—not exactly an occasion that calls for your best burgundy. Finish off the four-pack of Boddis.

INGREDIENTS

For best flavor, use a kosher roasting chicken. The recipe calls for Boddingtons, but any can of beer will work. Remember, though, as you head farther down the beer aisle (Coors Light, Milwaukee's Best, Natural Light) the dish becomes less and less presentable.

FOR THE BEER CAN
- 1 can of Boddingtons
- 1½ teaspoons salt
- ½ teaspoon paprika
- ¼ teaspoon cayenne
- ¼ teaspoon onion powder
- ½ teaspoon garlic powder
- ¼ teaspoon ground black pepper
- ¼ teaspoon dried thyme
- ¼ teaspoon dried oregano
- ¼ teaspoon dried sage
- 1 pinch of cumin

FOR THE CHICKEN
- 1 roasting chicken
- 3 tablespoons butter

Preparing the Chicken and Can

1. In a small bowl, combine herbs and spices to make spice mixture.
2. Open a can of Boddingtons and let it sit for one minute. Chug half the beer to make room for the spice mixture. Add half of the spice mixture to beer can. Swirl can to mix.
3. Rub interior and exterior of chicken with butter and remaining spice rub.
4. Place the can on the counter, grab chicken, and lower the chicken over the can. The can's open top should now be well inside the body cavity.

Grilling the Chicken

1. Place the grill 6 inches opposite the coals (try to simulate indirect heat).
2. Stand chicken on grill using base of can and chicken legs for support. Close grill cover and cook for about 70 minutes. Chicken will be done when juices drawn from thighs (use a knife) run clear.
3. Let chicken rest on a cutting board for 8 minutes before eating.

The Fuel Debate: Charcoal

So gas takes the lead when it comes to convenience and ease of grilling. Why bother with charcoal? Read on.

The Case for Charcoal: Convenience is nice, but it don't pull chicks. If it did, clip-on ties would replace your Brooks Brothers collection. Your date would swoon as you quoted Hemingway from *Reader's Digest*. And *Cheerleader Lesbians: New Recruits* would pass for a chick flick. Sadly, they won't, she won't, and it won't. Convincing chicks to sleep with you will always be a study in inconvenience.

The benefits of charcoal can be summed up in one phrase—high heat. When charcoal burns, it releases a greater amount of energy than gas, resulting in a higher temperature at the grilling surface. This higher temperature allows for grilled foods to be quickly seared, effectively caramelizing the surface and achieving that characteristic and much-sought-after charred flavor. With high heat the charring process occurs quickly, locking in flavorful juices that would otherwise be lost. And loss of your juices, mind you, should never happen before it's time.

Salads

Salad could turn out to be your ace in the hole. Girls love them, they're easy to put together, and they make a great short-notice snack or light meal. Plus they're guilt free—a huge factor when cooking for the always weight-obsessed female.

In the past, salad has gotten a bad rap as "sissy" food. The following recipes, however, boast bold flavors, and go better with a cold beer than a sparkling water. Make them with pride knowing that your manhood will not be sacrificed. Now, let's toss some salads.

T.G.'s Salad Dressing

The source of this recipe is a retired World War II sub-captain. He was married to a Miss America runner-up, and now, well into his eighties, still chases skirts like it's his job. Presumably, this dressing is to thank for his exploits. Consider it "chicks in a bottle."

 INGREDIENTS

The key to this dressing is the balsamic vinegar (see "Miracle Water," p. 128, for more info).

1 clove garlic, minced

½ shallot, minced

1½ cups vegetable oil

1 cup ketchup

1 cup balsamic vinegar

2 teaspoons Worcestershire sauce, or to taste

Salt and freshly ground black pepper to taste

1. Combine ingredients in a sealable container. Shake vigorously.
2. Place in refrigerator for 24 hours before serving.

Miracle Water

Over the years, vinegar has been sold as a hair softener, odor remover, and even a feminine hygiene product. Today a certain derivative of the acidic liquid, balsamic vinegar, can be used to help you get laid.

With its complex flavors, light acidity, and smooth sweetness, balsamic is truly an exquisite fluid. Made from the juice of Italy's Trebbino grape, balsamic is left to age in barrels of varying wood types and sizes until the desired flavor is reached. Prices can range from 20 cents to 40 dollars per ounce, with flavors ranging from heavily acidic to cherry, blackberry, and wine-like.

The uses for balsamic are virtually limitless—dip bread in it, use it as a marinade, and even drizzle it on strawberries for dessert. Regardless of how you use it, the majority of chicks will be taken by its flavor, and you'll have to tear them away from the bottle.

Best Salad Ever

Once you have a batch of T.G.'s dressing ready to go, make your chick this salad as a light meal or lunch. The title is no exaggeration, and she'll be asking you to make it again and again.

 DRINKS

If you're drinking wine, choose one with enough acidity to match the vinegar in the dressing.

Most any beer will go perfectly with this salad, but for some reason Anchor Steam pairs particularly well.

 INGREDIENTS

Make sure your bleu cheese will crumble (some brands are too soft). Make an effort to find an excellent, ripe tomato. Wash and thoroughly dry all ingredients before adding dressing.

½ head of romaine lettuce, torn into bite-sized pieces	½ cup garbanzo beans, drained
	½ cup kidney beans, drained
¼ cup chopped salami	1 avocado, diced
2 radishes, sliced thin	1 tomato, diced
3 green onions, chopped	3 ounces crumbled bleu cheese

Bring ingredients together in a large serving bowl. Add homemade croutons (see page 131) and serve.

Salad Tips

Yes, salads are simple, but the following tips can make the difference between a successful salad and a dud.

- *Got wood?* Salad looks and tastes better when served in wooden bowls. Serve 'em if you got 'em.
- *Towel off.* After you wash your ingredients, pat them dry with a paper towel or place them in a salad dryer. Failing to do so will mean water in your salad, making for dull, bland flavors.
- *Get fresh.* Your salad will only be as good as your least fresh ingredient. Buy fresh and skip the lettuce in a bag, prepackaged carrots, etc.
- *Make it and serve it.* Every moment your salad spends hanging around does damage to its flavors and textures. Get it to the table as soon as possible.
- *Don't cut.* Tearing lettuce will help you avoid the brown edges that result from cutting leaves with a knife.
- *Chill.* Place the plates and silverware you'll be using in the fridge before serving. At the very least, avoid warm plates, as they will wilt the salad.

Croutons

The over-seasoned chunks of stale bread that are sold prepackaged in supermarkets will ruin your salad rather than help it. Instead, make the croutons yourself and return them to their rightful position as the best part of the salad.

 INGREDIENTS

Choose a good, artisan-quality loaf of bread (sourdough will do nicely). The better the quality of olive oil you use, the better the crouton will be.

2 cups of ½-inch cubes of good bread	½ teaspoon garlic salt
2 tablespoons extra virgin olive oil	Freshly ground black pepper to taste

1. Preheat oven to 400 degrees F.
2. Toss bread, oil, garlic salt, and pepper in an oven-safe dish or pie tin. Coat bread lightly with oil. If still dry, drizzle on more oil.
3. Bake, checking and stirring every 2 minutes, until golden brown and crunchy, about 7 minutes total.

Caprese Salad

Italian guys know a thing or two about charming chicks out of their knickers. They also know a thing or two about perfectly arranged flavors, a fact that is on full display when it comes to Caprese salad. Use it to drum up some *amore* on this side of the Atlantic.

🍷 DRINKS

Try a merlot both to match the acidity of the vinegar and to bring out the berry overtones possessed by many balsamics.

 INGREDIENTS

The ingredients are few, but vital. Finding a ripe tomato is a real challenge these days. Your best bet will be to shop while tomatoes are in season, perhaps at roadside fruit stands. As for the balsamic, a pricier vinegar than the one you dropped in the salad dressing would be a good idea. Last, and most important, make sure you're using *fresh* mozzarella, which comes packaged in water. Using standard, dry-packed mozzarella will give you a castrated, barely edible version of Caprese.

Fresh mozzarella (drained), one thin slice for every slice of tomato	2 tablespoons balsamic vinegar
	Salt and freshly ground black pepper to taste
2 large ripe tomatoes, sliced into ¼-inch-thick rounds	½ cup fresh basil leaves, torn into ¼-inch strips
3 tablespoons extra virgin olive oil	

1. Arrange slices of mozzarella on a large plate. Top each with a like-sized piece of tomato.
2. Drizzle olive oil and balsamic vinegar evenly over all. Add salt and pepper to taste.
3. Scatter basil leaves over the top. Serve with fresh bread.

Caesar Salad

Would you rather have an evening with Salma Hayek, or the recipe for Caesar salad? Before you answer with what seems like the obvious choice between these two finest of Mexican imports, consider the following parable: "Give a man a fish, and he eats for a day. Teach a man to fish, and he eats for a lifetime." Sure, an evening with Salma would be beyond memorable. But the recipe for a good Caesar is like a chick-lure, guaranteed to land you girl after girl.

 DRINKS

A sauvignon blanc will be nice, as would a cold bottle of the Mexican lager Pacifico Clara.

 INGREDIENTS

This recipe is a simple, *faux* version of Caesar. As such, the ingredients involve no surprises. Anchovy paste is easier to find than you might think, and does more for this salad than you realize. Don't skip it.

FOR THE DRESSING
- 3 cloves garlic, minced
- 1 cup olive oil, divided into two ½ cups
- 2 teaspoons anchovy paste
- 3 tablespoons bleu cheese dressing (good-quality bottled is fine)

Juice of 1 lemon
½ cup grated Parmesan cheese

FOR THE SALAD
- 1 head of romaine, washed and torn into bite-sized pieces
- Fresh croutons (see page 131)

1. In a small bowl, stir garlic and first ½ cup of olive oil together. Let sit for about 10 minutes, to allow garlic to infuse oil.

2. Add anchovy paste to garlic and oil. Fork the mixture together until an even consistency is reached.

3. Add bleu cheese, lemon juice, and Parmesan. Stir together.

4. While stirring, slowly add reserved oil until desired dressing consistency is reached (could be as little as one tablespoon, or as much as ½ cup). Do not over stir, as frothing may occur.

5. Add appropriate amount of dressing (not too much) to romaine and croutons. Toss and serve.

Dessert

Intense laboring in the kitchen, followed by the unveiling of a perfectly cooked steak, will have her marveling at your gentlemanly sensibilities. Intense laboring in the kitchen followed by the unveiling of a perfectly baked raspberry tart will have her wondering how she ended up with such a complete candy-ass. Desserts rank low on the masculinity scale, and you should be careful about how much effort you devote to them.

The two recipes that follow should keep you out of trouble. One involves leaping flames and the other tastes too good for anyone to notice how big of a sissy you are. Keep the portions small and don't linger too long at the dessert table—you've got more important things to do after dinner.

Bananas Foster

The thrown-together, lazy elegance of Bananas Foster will allow you to avoid looking like a dessert-obsessed fruit. The leaping flames won't hurt, either.

Aside from the obvious threat to life and property posed by the flambé, the greatest danger here is overcooking. When left too long, the bananas turn pasty and flavorless. To preserve the individual flavors of the ingredients, pull this dish off the stove sooner rather than later.

 DRINKS

The sweetness of most desserts will dull all but the sweetest of wines. Dessert wines, ice wines, or sherry will be among the few that can stand up for themselves.

Beer with dessert? Maybe. Try a Hefeweizen with a lemon wedge, or an apple cider.

 INGREDIENTS

Use the highest-quality ice cream possible. For the rum, try Myers's Dark.

3 tablespoons unsalted butter	¼ cup dark rum
½ cup brown sugar	½ pint vanilla ice cream
2 ripe bananas, peeled and sliced into ½-inch rounds	

Sautéeing the Bananas

1. Heat a frying pan over medium-high heat. When warm, add butter and swirl to coat sides.
2. When butter is melted, add brown sugar. Stir until sugar is dissolved.
3. Add bananas and cook until they just begin to brown.

Adding the Rum

1. Add the rum. Swirl the pan, allowing the rum to cover the bananas.
2. After 5 to 10 seconds of swirling, ignite the rum with a match. Keep all flammable materials (including your head) away from the flame.
3. When flame dies, remove from heat and serve.

Serving

Top two scoops of vanilla ice cream with the bananas. Spoon sauce from pan over both.

Sexual Chocolate

Chicks love dessert. In fact, they love it too damn much. Given a choice between you and dessert, she'll take the sweets almost every time. And like sexual tranquilizer darts, rich desserts leave chicks feeling blissful, relaxed, and completely satisfied, with no use for you.

When forced to produce a dessert, find an alternative to the double chocolate bliss sex-drive diffuser craved by so many otherwise virile women. Fresh berries and cream can hardly be beat. The Bananas Foster recipe on page 137 and the Tiramisu on the next page should do nicely as well. One hint: If whipped cream is on the menu, do the whipping yourself to avoid any sleazebag vibes generated by the Reddi-wip aerosol can (unless, of course, those sleazebag vibes are welcomed).

Tiramisu

With a longer ingredient list and more involved preparation, this dessert qualifies as an evening affair. The literal translation of *tirami-su* is "carry me up," with worshipers of the dessert claiming heaven to be the implied destination. With luck, you'll keep heaven waiting, and carry her straight up to bed.

 DRINKS

Coffee with a spot of brandy seems a nice choice. A dessert wine such as *vin santo* could also do the trick.

 INGREDIENTS

Mascarpone is a smooth Italian cheese that can be found in gourmet grocery stores. Make sure you bring it to room temperature before making the filling. The espresso can be brewed at home or ordered from a coffee shop and placed in the fridge. Use your choice of Italian or domestic brandies. Finally, cocoa powder is *not* the same as instant cocoa. Look for Ghirardelli or Scharffen Berger brand cocoa powder.

FOR THE ESPRESSO SAUCE
- ½ cup granulated sugar
- ⅓ cup water
- ⅔ cup espresso coffee
- ¼ cup brandy

FOR THE FILLING
- ¾ cups heavy cream
- 3 tablespoons sugar
- 1¼ teaspoons vanilla
- ½ pound mascarpone cheese

FOR THE CAKE
- ¼ pound ladyfingers

FOR FINISHING
- Cocoa powder

Making the Sauce

1. Combine sugar and water in a saucepan over medium heat. Stir sugar into water until dissolved. Remove from heat when liquid begins to simmer.
2. When syrup is cooled, mix in coffee and brandy. Set aside.

Making the Filling

1. With an electric hand-mixer, whip the cream with sugar and vanilla until the mixture forms soft peaks.
2. Use a spatula to fold cream into mascarpone. (Folding, unlike mixing, will keep the cream light and fluffy.)

Bringing It Together

1. In a 2-quart baking dish, form a layer of ladyfingers. Drizzle enough sauce to soak the fingers, about half of the syrup.
2. Spread half of the mascarpone filling evenly over the top of the layer of lady fingers.
3. Repeat procedure with another layer of fingers, remaining syrup, and remaining mascarpone. Smooth top with a spatula. Refrigerate until ready to serve. Will keep in the refrigerator for 12 hours or so.
4. Before cutting, dust top layer with cocoa powder.
5. Serve 3" × 3" squares on small plates that have been dusted with powder. For extra effect, garnish with a few chocolate-covered coffee beans.

Bake It Like a Man?

Briefly: Pies, cookies, cakes, tarts, pastries, and anything else you might find at an elementary school bake sale are off-limits to any guy hoping to impress women. Real men don't bake sweets . . . or at least not when any single women are looking.

◆ Breakfast ◆
in Bed

Ostensibly, she's already in your bed. Cooking for her now seems (to most practical gentlemen) like waling away on a long-since-dead horse. And so, before cracking an egg or squeezing an orange, we must ask ourselves, "What exactly are we trying to accomplish here?" If the answer isn't "Showing her that I love her," put the eggs down and back away slowly.

In terms of relationship seriousness, breakfast in bed ranks somewhere between introducing her to your parents and choosing baby names. If the girl in question is a long-term investment, by all means grab the lap tray and some fresh flowers. If not, your job is to get her off your property, pronto. Once that's done, skip ahead to the drink section and plan your afternoon.

The Mimosa

Elegant brunch refreshment, or thinly veiled excuse to booze before 10 a.m.? The mimosa is both, and that's why it ranks somewhere between ESPN Classic and the halter top as one of man's great creations. Serve it with either of the recipes in this section. A quick hint, though—do not offer her a mimosa right after she's brushed her teeth. The combination of citrus, champagne, and toothpaste is enough to make anyone cringe.

 INGREDIENTS

Making a mimosa with frozen OJ and Cook's Champagne will have your lips puckering and salivary glands aching. For a truly great experience, get hold of fresh squeezed juice and pair it with a reasonably good champagne, such as Veuve Clicquot.

Fresh orange juice, chilled   Grand Marnier liqueur
Champagne, chilled

Making a Mimosa

Simple. Fill half of a champagne glass with orange juice. Fill the second half with champagne and a splash of Grand Marnier. Serve cold.

Swedish Pancakes

Once you decide to go ahead with the B.I.B., pull out all the stops. Fresh flowers, fresh-squeezed orange juice, and fresh-brewed coffee are good places to start. For the full effect, invest in a bed tray, and keep her in bed as long as possible.

To that end, these light, thin pancakes will have her begging for seconds. They're great with butter and syrup, or can be paired with more elaborate toppings such as fruit compote and whipped cream. Fry some bacon or sausage to complete the meal.

 DRINKS

In the morning? You bet. Check the recipe preceding these pancakes for the king of breakfast booze—mimosa.

 INGREDIENTS

Pretty simple. The topping can be just about anything you want. If you're going with syrup, however, use fresh maple and skip the Log Cabin/Aunt Jemima scene.

3 eggs	2 teaspoons salt
1 quart whole milk	Powdered sugar
¼ pound butter	Syrup, fruit compote, or jam for topping
1¾ cups all-purpose flour	

Making the Batter

1. In a large mixing bowl, slowly blend eggs and milk until an even consistency is reached.
2. Place a nonstick skillet over medium-high heat. Add butter.
3. Add flour and salt to mixture. Stir until flour is completely incorporated.
4. When butter is melted in skillet, add it to the batter. Whisk vigorously until smooth.

Cooking the Pancakes

1. Lower the heat under the skillet to medium.
2. When pan is hot, add a small ladle of batter (about ⅓ cup) to the pan. Swirl to spread batter evenly across bottom of skillet.
3. When brown, turn pancake with a spatula. Do so with one smooth motion and a flip of the wrist, so as to avoid tearing.
4. When the second side is covered with brown spots, remove it from the pan.
5. Lay the pancake flat on a plate. Butter it while open, then roll it end to end. Serve with syrup, jam, or fruit compote.

Eggs Benedict

If you burned off some calories the night before, there's no better way of replacing them than with eggs benedict. English muffins topped with Canadian bacon and drowned in hollandaise sauce are the epitome of decadence, and you'll probably want to climb back in bed for a nap when you're finished.

 DRINKS

Mimosa, baby, mimosa.

 INGREDIENTS

You can drive yourself crazy trying to get hollandaise made from scratch to come out right. Instead, take the easy road and use a packaged mix. It tastes every bit as good as real hollandaise and saves you the hassle. Try the mix from Knorr (you'll find it at the supermarket).

FOR THE HOLLANDAISE SAUCE
- 1 package Knorr hollandaise mix
- Butter
- Milk
- Lemon
- 1 tablespoon chopped parsley

FOR THE BACON, EGGS, AND MUFFINS
- ½ tablespoon butter
- 4 slices Canadian bacon
- 4 large, fresh eggs
- Water
- 2 toasted English muffins, plain

Making the Hollandaise Sauce

Follow the directions on the package. Keep warm on back burner for later use. Right before serving, add parsley to sauce.

Frying the Bacon

1. Place a small skillet over medium-high heat. Add butter to pan, and swirl to coat sides.
2. Add bacon to pan. Fry for 1 minute on each side, just until hot.

Poaching the Eggs

1. Fill a large sauté pan with water to a depth of about 3 inches. Place the pan over high heat and bring to a boil. Once water is boiling, reduce heat and maintain a slow simmer.
2. Crack each egg and slide into the simmering water. Poach each egg for 3 to 5 minutes or until the whites are cooked, turning every minute or so with a spoon.

Serving

Toast English muffins and top each with one slice of bacon and a poached egg. Spoon hollandaise sauce over all.

Drinks

We can all remember our early experiences with chicks and booze. As long as the girls had a pulse and the drinks were saccharine sweet, we knew everything was going to turn out right. Boone's Farm, Bartles + Jaymes, and peach schnapps with orange juice ruled the day. Drinking like a man meant vodka in Snapple or lukewarm forties of Woodchuck Cider. Life was simple, drinks were sweet, and the girls were easy.

All good things, however, come to an end, and the time for raising your booze IQ has come. In this final (and arguably most important) chapter, we will engage in a crash-course of liquor knowledge. The goal is not to graduate with your bartender's license, but rather to walk away with a hit-list of simple drinks you can use to woo women. So put the Zima down, and remove the cocktail umbrella from behind your ear. It's time to get serious about your drink.

Vodka

The drink of choice for rosy-cheeked Russians, homeless people, and cell-phone addicted posers in Prada pants, vodka is a flexible and useful spirit to have around the house. The good thing about vodka (or the bad thing, depending on where you stand) is that it's basically flavorless. This means that it will coalesce with a wide variety of mixers, and allow other flavors in the drink to take command. To elevate it from utility guy to superstar, however, just shell out a few extra bucks for a premium brand. The frosted/mirrored/painted packaging alone will have her thinking you're a jet-setting sophisticate.

WHAT YOU'RE DRINKING

Vodka is made from wheat, barley, rye, or potatoes that have been fermented, distilled, filtered, and diluted. The ultra-trendy spirit has humble Eastern European origins, but premium brands are now distilled in locales ranging from France to the United States. Premium brands are fairly indistinguishable from one another beyond fancy packaging.

THE MESSAGE

"I'm a shaker and a mover. At any moment someone important might call, and I'll be outta here. You probably should sleep with me before that happens."

The Cosmopolitan

A Drink for Her

A classic vodka cocktail? There aren't many, but the Cosmopolitan is the matriarch of the family.

 INGREDIENTS

2 ounces vodka	1 ounce lime juice
2 ounces cranberry juice	½ ounce Cointreau

Mix ingredients with ice. Strain and serve "up" (sans ice) in a martini glass. Garnish with lime peel.

Vodka Collins

A Drink for Him

By fixing yourself this old standby, you're not only showing her that you respect a classic, you're helping wage a war against that bastard child, the vodka tonic.

 INGREDIENTS

2½ ounces vodka	1 teaspoon sugar
1 ounce lemon juice	2 ounces soda water

Mix vodka, lemon juice, and sugar in a shaker with crushed ice. Strain into a collins glass (a tall, 8-ounce glass) over ice cubes. Top with 2 ounces of soda water.

Bloody Mary

A Drink for the Next Morning

Revered as a hangover cure, the bloody mary is an exceptional way to start the morning. Who knows, if you and your morning guest bag two of these apiece, you'll probably end up right back where you started—in bed with a pleasant buzz.

 INGREDIENTS

2 ounces vodka

4 ounces tomato juice

½ ounce lemon juice

8 drops Worcestershire Sauce

4 drops Tabasco Sauce

¼ teaspoon fresh horseradish, grated

Celery salt to taste

Freshly ground black pepper to taste

Mix ingredients and pour into a collins glass (a tall, 8-ounce glass) over ice. Garnish with a thinly sliced celery stick.

Gin

Any spirit with devotees from Winston Churchill to Snoop Dogg must have something special. From colonial watering holes in malaria-stricken lands to the high-style martini bars of Manhattan, gin rules on the basis of its unique, refreshing flavor. As a contributing partner in your quest to pull chicks, gin can provide you with instant credibility as a man who respects tradition and recognizes the value in simple elegance. First, however, you'll have to lose that twisted "I'm drinking a christmas tree" facial expression.

WHAT YOU'RE DRINKING

Gin begins as a neutral spirit made from grain that is then flavored with any number of botanicals (juniper, coriander, citrus) with juniper berry always used in the greatest proportion. Distinctively English, nearly all premium gins are distilled in the British Isles. Common origin doesn't, however, lead to common character. There is a wide variety of gin recipes, each with distinctive flavors and subtleties. Get a taste of the old guard with Plymouth or Beefeater gins. For an update on the classic, go with Bombay Sapphire.

THE MESSAGE

"I'm a classic. My preferences are distinctive. I asked you to dinner because I see that you are a woman of substance. I'll gladly drive you home in my Aston Martin . . . in the morning, that is."

The Singapore Sling

A Drink for Her

As chick-drink as gin gets.

 **INGREDIENTS**

1½ ounces gin	½ ounce creme de cassis
½ ounce cherry brandy	¼ ounce grenadine
½ ounce lemon juice	¾ ounce soda water
½ ounce lime juice	

Mix all ingredients except the soda with ice. Stir to blend. Top with soda water and serve.

The Gibson

A Drink for Him

Of course, if gin is on the menu, you should be drinking a martini. The Gibson is a classic that forgoes the standard olive on a skewer for two pickled pearl onions.

 INGREDIENTS

2½ ounces gin	2 cocktail onions
¼ ounce dry vermouth	

Mix gin and vermouth over ice. Strain into a martini glass and garnish with onion.

The Clover Club

A Drink to Reminisce With

This cocktail isn't so much a classic as it is a dinosaur. One taste of this creamy concoction, and you'll see why it should be revived.

 **INGREDIENTS**

1½ ounces gin	¾ ounce lemon juice
½ ounce grenadine	1 egg white

Shake ingredients with ice. Strain into a chilled glass.

Whiskey

With more variety than a Tijuana brothel, there's a whiskey for every man, woman, and occasion. Scotch, Tennessee, Bourbon, Irish—the list goes on. Take the time to taste a wide assortment of this spirit, settle on the label that suits you, and make it your permanent whiskey wing-man. Know when to say when, as taking the train too far can leave you, as the saying goes, with a serious case of "whiskey Dick Nixon."

WHAT YOU'RE DRINKING

There are as many ways to make whiskey as there are varieties. The basic thread is to take grain, corn, or a blend of the two, ferment and distill it, then leave it to age in barrels. These barrels impart much of the flavor, and anything from used sherry casks to charred oak can be utilized.

THE MESSAGE

"I'm a healthy blend of southern gentleman, Scottish nobleman, and lonesome cowboy. All three of these personalities would be mighty obliged if you would sleep with us."

Whiskey Lemonade

A Drink for Her

Nothing classic about it, but she'll love the taste. Perfect for a summer evening.

 **INGREDIENTS**

2 ounces blended whiskey	4½ ounces club soda
1 ounce lemon juice	1 maraschino cherry
1 teaspoon sugar	

Mix ingredients and pour over crushed ice. Garnish with cherry.

The Old Fashioned

A Drink for Him

Though bourbon or rye seem to work best, almost any whiskey should fit in this cocktail.

 INGREDIENTS

2 dashes of bitters	1 strip orange peel
1 teaspoon sugar	Splash of soda water
2 ounces whiskey	

In the bottom of a short glass, stir bitters and sugar until an even consistency is reached. Add whiskey, orange peel, and ice. Top with soda water.

Irish Coffee

A Drink for In Front of the Fireplace

With a fire raging, you'll need a hot drink. When you finish the second one, ask if you can "slip into someone more comfortable."

 **INGREDIENTS**

4 ounces fresh brewed coffee	1 ounce Irish whiskey
1 teaspoon sugar	1 ounce heavy cream

Heat glass with hot water (that way the drink will stay hot). Pour water out and add coffee and sugar, stirring to dissolve sugar. Add whiskey, then cream.

The Rest of the Field

The big three of vodka, gin, and whiskey are tough to beat. Tradition and taste are solidly in their court. But there are moments and occasions that call for something a bit different. When the mood is right, pull one of these dark-horse spirits off the bench, and send them into the game. The opposition won't know what hit her.

Rum

When choosing a mentor for your chick-pulling escapades, the sailor on shore leave should not be emulated. His liquor, however, can come along.

Made from sugar cane that has been fermented and either aged (for dark) or not (for silver), a good rum drink should conjure images of sandy beaches and crystal blue ocean waters. It should not, however, strip you of your manhood and self respect. Rum is a notorious base for the "chick-drink," and any recipe you consider should be screened for estrogen content. If she's snickering, you know you chose wrong.

The Hemingway Daiquiri

A Drink to Watch the Sunset With

This isn't the neon-colored, frozen eyesore served at your local T.G.I. Friday's. This is a proper cocktail conceived by none other than Ernest Hemingway. Considering he drove an ambulance in World War I and shagged nurses like it was his patriotic duty, his cocktail won't damage your measly chances one bit.

INGREDIENTS

1½ ounces rum   ¾ ounce lime juice
¼ ounce maraschino cherry   ¼ ounce grapefruit juice
   juice

Mix ingredients over ice. Strain into a chilled glass.

Tequila

Almost all girls have a story about how the evening started with tequila and ended with them on their knees . . . puking, that is. Tequila on your romantic evening may be a tough sell at first. Begin by assuring them that high-quality tequila is as harmless as a baby bird. Finish by mixing them the drink that follows.

The Margarita

A Drink to Celebrate Cinco de Mayo With

Again, not the giant slurpee you're probably familiar with. The margarita is best when served on the rocks, rather than through a blender. The salt is optional, while excellent tequila is not. Try Herradura Silver for the best results.

INGREDIENTS

1½ ounces silver tequila   1 ounce lime
1 ounce cointreau   Salt
1 ounce lemon juice

Mix ingredients with ice. Strain and serve on the rocks in a salt-rimmed glass (rub the rim with lime and dip in kosher salt).

Brandy

Tastes best when wearing a smoking jacket, slippers, and three buxom blondes. Barring that, brandy can be imbibed on one of your more formal forays. If she's dressed nicely, and if you can cook while mildly intoxicated, start the evening off, and end it, with a trip to the brandy bottle.

The Sidecar

A Drink to Loosen Your Tie With

Cognac is prized by many as the Cadillac of spirits. One taste of a good bottle, and you'll start to see why. This drink puts brandy's best foot forward, and will make her sweet, sour, and warm all over.

 **INGREDIENTS**

1½ ounces cognac   ¾ ounces lemon juice
 ¾ ounces cointreau

Rub the rim of a cocktail glass with lemon, then dip it in extra-fine sugar. Mix ingredients with ice, and strain into sugared glass.

Resource Guide

For the perfect sauté pan, or chef's knife, or squeeze bottle (as mentioned in the section on presentation), or any other kitchen utensil, check out your local Sur la Table or Williams-Sonoma. These stores stock just about every piece of cooking hardware you can imagine, and even hold in-store cooking classes and demonstrations. And as if that weren't enough, on a daily basis they play host to a plentitude of wealthy, sexually unsatisfied divorcées just waiting to be hit on. If you can't find a store near you, order a catalog and have your goods shipped (as of this printing, the divorcées are not available by mail).

For a bottle of Plymouth Gin delivered right to your door, head to www.bevmo.com. With thousands of beers, wines, and spirits available at a mouse click, Bevmo is the Amazon.com of booze. Bar accessories are available as well.

For a tube of wasabi paste, or any other hard-to-find ingredient, log on to www.earthydelights.com. Specializing in exotic produce, this site will save you a potential goose chase for ingredients such as wild mushrooms or truffle oil. As an added bonus, the site also features edible flowers including orchids, sprouting peas, and squash blossoms. Who knew garnish could get you laid?

For great cooking advice, visit websites like <u>www.epicurious.</u> <u>com</u>. With a wealth of information on tap, Epicurious will provide an answer to most any culinary question you may have. If the answer still eludes you, head to a forum and ask the masses for some help. Or stop by "Gail's Recipe Swap" to expand your repertoire. Don't, however, be misled by Gail's tag-line, "We'll show you ours if you show us yours." Nude photos get deleted pretty fast . . . not that we'd know anything about that.

For an outdoor grill, you could go to a grill dealer and get a fancy, 400-dollar gas behemoth. But why? Head to your local Wal-Mart or G.I. Joe's and pick up a run-of-the-mill charcoal grill. For 1/10th the cost, you can generate some serious heat for searing steaks and fish. It would be nice to say these department stores are also great places to pick up chicks. Alas, beautiful women are rarely found under the same roof as fishing gear, electronics, and automotive supplies.

For a free cooking lesson, tune in to Food Network. There is no substitute for watching great chefs in action. You'll pick up knife moves, solid ingredient advice, and a little wine knowledge to boot. Plus you'll find that, in addition to being cold, greedy, and snobbish, Martha Stewart is disturbingly sexy.

For candles, barware, threads, or anything else you need to woo women, check out Urban Outfitters. Few merchants offer such a wide variety of materials designed to help you get laid. If the military had a chick-hunting division, this place would be its surplus store. Also, the fact that U.O. sells a ready-made beer-pong court can only be seen as a positive.

For a new recipe head to your local bookseller. Expanding your cooking library will have a direct effect on your ability as a budding chef. Places like Barnes and Noble, Borders, or Powell's have extensive cookbook collections and comfy chairs in which to give them a browsing.

Cooking publications such as *Saveur, Cook's Illustrated, Food and Wine, Gourmet,* and others will also provide you with a wealth of information. Grab a few subscriptions, and let inspiration arrive every month.

For dishes to cook with, and bedding to . . . er . . . bed on, visit Bed Bath and Beyond or Crate and Barrel. These superstores have everything you need to build a love nest. Cookware, tableware, housewares, it's all there. Now all you need is a chick.

For a true chef's hub on the web, steer your browser to www. cooks.com. Recipes, advice, and links to cooking resources are on tap. Of particular usefulness is the "unit calculator" which quickly converts recipes from metric to English units or vice versa (yes, you can calculate how hung you're not in Europe).

For the best place to buy cookbooks online, load up www. ecookbooks.com, a.k.a. Jessica's Biscuit. With its cookbook reviews, recipes, and even posters, ecookbooks has so much to offer, you'll quickly get over your disappointment at the lack of attention given to the actual "biscuit." But you never know—with a little encouragement, Jessica might just warm up to the idea.

For cookware delivered to your door visit www.chefscatalog. com or www.cooking.com. All the top brands of cookware (All-Clad, Le Creuset, KitchenAid, etc.) are there, as well as a few that are easier on the wallet (Calphalon, for instance). Quality knives like Henckels and Wüsthof are also available for order. Check the clearance sections for the best deals around.

Some Metric Equivalents
(for Quick Reference)

Volume

The following metric equivalents are slightly larger, but results will not be affected (just scant the measurements a bit).

1 gallon	=	4 liters
1 quart	=	1 liter
1 pint	=	500 ml
1 cup	=	250 ml

Note: "1 8-ounce can" equals 1 cup

The following metric equivalents are slightly smaller (be a bit generous with the measurements).

1 tablespoon	=	15 ml
1 teaspoon	=	5 ml

Weight

1 pound	=	450 g (approx. ½ kilo)
1 ounce	=	28 g

Note: 1 tablespoon of butter equals 15 grams
1 cup of flour equals 140 grams
1 cup of sugar equals 200 grams

Length

1 inch	=	2.5 cm

Oven Temperatures

"Cool" = 250°–275° F	=	120°–135° C	gas mark (regulo)	= ½–1
"Moderate" = 350° F	=	175° C		= 4
"Hot" = 425°–450° F	=	220°–230° C		= 7–8

Index

About the Author

Garth Fuller was born and raised on a cattle ranch in Ellensburg, Washington. He attended Cornell University, captained their soccer team, and began to experiment with the "game-increasing effects" of cooking for chicks. Upon graduation in 2000, Garth took a position with Sur La Table, a chef's supply store. There, free access to cooking classes and significant discounts on cooking gadgets helped him sharpen his skills. Today, Garth splits his time equally between writing, surfing, and cooking great meals for the women of Los Angeles.